Well I'm Blowed

- would you believe it!

More than

1000 Words and Sayings

heard within a stone's throw of

'Pompey' and 'Turktown'

in the 1930's to early 1950's.

Some forgotten, others rarely heard,
many still in use today.

Published as a companion to

The way it was - more or less!

First Edition published in October 2007
by
Denfbee Publishing
Haysel House, Paxford, Chipping Campden
Gloucestershire GL55 6XL

Telephone: 01386 593 435
email: denfbee@aol.com

ISBN 978-0-9556665-0-6

Designed and printed
by
STUDIO 6
The Square, Wickham, Hampshire PO17 5JN

Telephone: 01329 832933
www.studio-6.co.uk

Well I'm Blowed

- would you believe it!

- is for my
Family and Friends

and all those writers and readers
who enjoy having a way with words

Acknowledgements

My grateful thanks go to:

All those 'Old Gosportians' and 'Portmuthians'
whose suggestions added many a local word and saying.

Frank Hawkhead for his encouragement in the early stages,
and to Kate for wise counsel at key stages.

Leo the landlord of the 'Churchill Arms', Paxford for his discovery
of the word Cadigan.

The staff at
The Gosport Discovery Centre and Local Studies Section
and The Portsmouth Central Reference Library
and Local Studies Section.

Alison Gardiner for her evocative illustrations and Helen Palacz
whose diligent reading righted many a wrong,
and by no means least to Joyce for a wife's forbearance.

Contents

Preamble

Once upon a time, when going places was once a year and not too far away, remembering choice words and sayings spoken by the locals would bring to life many a silent 'snap'.

The language we use to communicate is continually changing. The active life of words and sayings is seemingly determined by a constant compulsion for change. Fuelled by multi-culturalism and TV in a world described by Marshall McLuhan, in his book, 'The Gutenberg Galaxy' as a 'global village'.

Idioms, buzz-words and clichés are all too easily swept aside by society's insatiable appetite for what's new, even to the extent of using five words when one will do. For example, when will 'at this moment in time' be superseded by a single word such as 'now,' and 'cool' be replaced by another word meaning OK?

Nothing breathes more realism and vitality into recalling the past than by using the words and sayings of yesterday. As such they deserve to be cherished and preserved as icons of one's never to be forgotten youth.

I acknowledge my late Father 'Fred', as a prime practitioner in the use of these words and sayings, and who has unwittingly provided a foundation upon which this book is based. It could be said that he has *much to answer for*. On the other hand, I much prefer to celebrate them in his memory.

Was it merely a consequence of being brought up to be seen and not heard that gave me an ever listening ear, and a memory bank of voices that appear on these pages as words and sayings? Hopefully they will also be of interest and use to students of all ages pursuing linguistic, social and local history studies.

Finally may this compilation tickle the fancy of my contemporaries and for all and sundry, promote an interest in probing the past with words.

Dennis Boxall
Paxford
September 2007

Introduction

- By looking up the Index of Themes (Part One), and then the words and sayings under those themes (Part Two), individual words and sayings with their meanings in the A - Z (Part Four) should be easier to find.

- More Words and Sayings can be found lurking in the columns of meanings, bringing the number of entries in the A - Z to well over 1000. *Even so, there are many more waiting to be discovered and recorded.*

- The choice of Words and Sayings, their spelling and their meanings are entirely those of the author. Other interpretations are not only possible, but may be equally valid.

- Those entries in the A - Z that appear in bold UPPERCASE type are taken from the Selected Words and Sayings (Part Three). For example, 'Alverstocracy', 'Chish and Fips', 'Heading north over Portsdown Hill', 'Turktown' and 'Pompey' etc., have been chosen as descriptive of the 'times', and are also used throughout the telling of the *The Way it Was - more or less*

- The origins and derivations of 'Pompey' and 'Turktown' together with links to the origins of many other words and sayings may be found in Sources of Further Reference on pages 137-140.

- A linguistic study of Part One to Part Four may reveal insights into the way things were, and the way life was in the 1930's-1950's. For example some entries listed under a particular theme may contain clues to the behaviour and social norms of the day.

- Please note that no claim is made nor intention implied that these words and sayings have only been heard in, or stem from Gosport and Portsmouth. *On the other hand there are many that can be rightly and proudly described as truly local.*

The illustration on the back cover captioned
and we called them the 'ARZUMS' was what
us'ens called our playground that bordered
the muddy tide worn banks of Forton Creek.

Part One

Index of Themes
with Part Two page numbers

Part Two

Words and Sayings arranged by Theme

with Part Four page numbers

Local Lingo

Father's Favourites

Words and Sayings by Theme

(A full list of Cadigans can be found on page 42)

Children & the Young

Choice

G

Games, Contest & Pastimes

Good & Bad

Greetings, Hellos & Goodbyes

H

Happiness & Unhappiness

Cadigans

- are words used on the spur of the moment when you can't think of the right one.

A whatnot	Oojaa
A whatsit	Oojameflick
A bloke	Oozelum bird
Blogs	So and so
Buggins	The 'doings'
Doo daa	Thingy
Doofer	Thing a me
Duberry	Thing a me bob
Farnsbarnes	Thing a me jig
Gladstone Fingelfaffer	Thingummy
Gubbins	You know! What's 'is name
Jobby	

Part Three

Selected Words & Sayings
with Part Four page numbers

Part Four

A to Z of Words and Sayings

'It won't ackle'

ABDABS	A dose of the jitters, see 'screaming abdabs'.
A blinkin', bloomin', cryin' shame	Ways of saying regrettable, terrible, what a pity.
A blot	An eyesore, e.g. 'on the landscape', or an unsightly blob of ink spilt on a page.
A bodge or bodge up	Workmanship of a poor standard, not up to scratch.
A BONNY	A bonfire.
Abracadabra	A magic word of command.
A bright spark	A clever person, above average, will go far.
ABYSSINIA	A farewell I'll be seeing you.
Acetylene	A fuel used in household lamps, and bicycle lamps before batteries.
A Charlie Noble	Chimney for a small stove.
A chit or chitty	A small form or permit.
ACKLE	Work, function, e.g. it won't ackle, means it won't work.
Action stations	Father's order to get going, get cracking, an urgent call to do something quickly.
A carry on	A to-do, a right carry on, a dust-up, untoward events, no not cabin luggage.
A cut above	Better than, superior to.
Adam's ale	Fresh drinking water.

Addled	A confused mental state, or an unfertile bird's egg.
A ding dong	A noisy altercation, a fracas.
A DOCKYARD OYSTER	A product of the disgusting habit of spitting on the ground.
A dog's dinner or a pig's breakfast	A bit of a mess to say the least.
A dust up	A bust up, argument, a row to send the feathers flying, or make the fur fly.
A flash in the pan	Short lived, destined to fail, not likely to succeed.
AFTERS	Pudding, sweet, dessert. 'What's for afters?'
After you Cecil, no after you Claude	A popular catchphrase that 'made a play' on being over and excessively polite.
A gammy leg	Lame, limp, or an injured leg.
A Godsend	Something of great benefit, so welcome a gift it could have come from heaven.
A good hiding	To physically chastise, to inflict corporal punishment, a beating up, e.g. a hiding to nothing.
A goner	Referring to something or someone who has disappeared or died.
A GOZZUNDER	An enamel or china 'jerry', 'po' or 'piss pot' that goes under the bed.
A jot	Nothing, not even a tiny bit, e.g. 'He couldn't care a jot'.
A lash up	Of a poor standard, but doing the best with what's available, and maybe the best that was possible in the circumstances.
A LICK OF PAINT	A one coat job for decorating the house or the complexion of a lady.
A little dicky bird told me	A tit bit received in confidence, or on the 'QT'.
Alive and kicking	Healthily active, as in a new born babe, or as in old age. Also said when confirming someone is alive, when the opposite was expected.
All above board	Open, honest, legit.
All at sea	Confused, disorientated not knowing which way to turn or tack.

All baloney	Total rubbish, nonsense, so much hot air, piffle, tosh.
All clear	A clean bill of health, or air raid sirens sounding the end of the warning of an air attack.
All along	Another way of saying 'all the time' e.g. he knew all the time or he knew all along.
ALL DOLLED UP	Looking one's best, dressed up to the 'nines', dressed to kill.
All done and dusted	Something completely and satisfactorily finished, over and done with, spic and span.
ALL DONE BY MIRRORS	Something achieved by magic, illusion, trickery or deception.
All ears	Listening attentively, paying attention, e.g. "I'm all ears".
Alleys	Coloured glass marbles.
All het up	Upset, hot and bothered, flustered.
All my eye and Betty Martin	Utter nonsense rubbish, unbelievable, balderdash.
All of a tizzy and all of a doodah	Flustered, confused, in a bit of a state, in a tizzwas.
All over the shop	Missing the mark by miles, all over the place, at sixes and sevens.
All square	The game finished up with nobody owing anybody anything, evenly matched, a draw, 'even stevens'.
All steamed up	Upset, hot and bothered, irate, on one's high horse.
ALVERSTOCRACY	Residents of Alverstoke, the so called 'up market' district of Gosport.
Alverstocrat	An 'aristocratic' resident of Alverstoke.
Ammo	Ammunition for toy guns e.g. caps. Nothing to do with the declension of the Latin verb to love.
An ACME or Mangle	A popular make of wringer, used for squeezing excess water out of the washing.
An alert	Another name for an air raid warning, like 'the sirens'.
And not before time	Meaning you're late in arriving or delivering something.
An 'erb	A scruffy little boy, see a right little 'erbert, short for Herbert.

ANNO DOMINI	The end of the road - metaphorically speaking and
Anno Domini	n. colloq. advancing age, and suffering from it.
Answering a call of nature	Another way of saying going to the toilet, going for a 'pee', or going for a 'slash'.
ANTIMACASSAR	Material put on chair backs to prevent greasy marks left by men using Brylcreem, or Brilliantine on their hair.
ANYRATE OR ANYWAY	To continue, continuing the story where you left off, or after an interruption, notwithstanding.
Ants in your pants	Fidgety, agitated, can't keep still, suffering from a dose of St.Vitus' dance.
'A packet of chips to grease your lips, out goes one, out goes another one, then out goes you'	A song with many variations e.g. a penn'th of chips sung by children when playing a game of elimination.
A piece of cake	Something easily done, a doddle, a walk over.
Arf er mo	Just you wait a moment, not so fast, hold on for a bit, hold yer horses.
ARGY BARGY	Verbal fuss and bother, and maybe pushing and shoving arising from a dispute.
A RIGHT OW'S YER FATHER	A way of saying it's a bit of a mess, a difficult situation, in a 'pickle', or a 'dust up'.
A right little 'erbert	A ragamuffin, a little scruff, a street urchin, an 'erb.
Arse about face	Back to front, wrong way round e.g. putting the cart before the horse.
ARZUMS	Rough undulating ground on the banks of Forton Creek, where children played war games. Our Never Never Land.
A screw loose	Somebody not all there, crazy, deficient in the 'grey matter'.
As good as gold	Butter wouldn't melt in 'is mouth, junior being given the benefit of the doubt by adoring parents.
A slow coach	Someone who shillies and shallies, dillies and dallies, taking a long time to do anything, is painfully slow.
ASPIDISTRA	An ornamental pot plant with large green leaves and no flowers, very popular for 'showing off' in the front room window to passers-by.

A square	Someone who won't take risks, cautious, fights shy of adventures and high jinks, a kill-joy.
As quick as a flash	Denoting speed, of short duration, over in a trice.
As right as rain	Fully restored to good health, and feeling fine.
As sure as eggs is eggs	A certainty, a dead cert.
As sure as God made little apples	To be sure, another expression of certainty.
A stony silence	An eerie, cold, absence of any sound, silence with a cause, silence with disdain.
Astronomical	Used to emphasise a sense of being enormous, or high, e.g. hit the roof, hit the ceiling, or describing house prices.
A swizz	To be tricked, something you have been tricked into doing, believing, or buying.
A tall order	To be given a difficult or unreasonable task to carry out.
A tall story	A tale not to be believed, or to be taken with a pinch of salt.
A tea fanny	A copper kettle of varying size used for brewing tea.
A TIMOTHY WHITES	Neither one thing nor t'other, a rag-bag, all-sorts, all things to all men, e.g. a timothy allsorts.
A to do	A kerfuffle, a social upset, a bit of a mix up, a domestic 'scene'
At a rate of knots	Speeding along, in a hurry, not necessarily in a ship at sea.
At sixes and sevens	In a muddle, confused and perplexed, all at sea.
Attaboy	Approval and encouragement.
At the drop of a hat	Responding quickly, instantly, or immediately, and without question.
At the end of your tether	Had enough, at your wits end, reached your limit, nearly done for, stretched to the limit, flaked out.
A turn up for the book	Something unexpected, a pleasant surprise.
Austerity	The word used to describe conditions of life in wartime resulting from shortages of food and materials.
A weather eye	Always on the lookout for portents of change e.g., the weather, and the future, hence 'coming events cast their shadows before'.

A whatnot, or whatsit   What you call something when you cannot remember the right name for it, known as a Cadigan.

A yacker and yackety yack   He or she who speaks endlessly and with little point or meaning, yackety-yack being what is said.

'Bless 'is little cotton socks'

BACCY	Pipe tobacco, e.g. the saying by pipe smokers, 'pipe, baccy and matches'.
Backsliding	Not pulling your weight, falling behind with whatever you were supposed to be doing.
Bad hat	A scoundrel, a good for nothing, ne're do well, has a reputation for persistent wrongdoing.
Bag	To claim or assert a wish or a right, (see 'its in the bag').
Bagged	Asserted a right to, or possession of something, or having shot an animal or game bird.
BAGS I	Assert a priority e.g. 'Bags I go first'.
Bags	Another word for trousers, or specifically referring to old, worn and 'baggy' trousers. Then there are 'old bags' that do not refer to trousers!
Bags of	More than enough, oodles of it, sufficient, plenty, e.g. 'there's bags of room'.
BAKELITE	An early form of plastic widely used as an alternative to glass, china, brass, e.g. for cups, picnic sets, ash trays and radio cabinets.
Bamboozle	Hoodwink, deceive, confuse, mislead, browbeat.
BAMPAA AND BAMPAM	Names for Grandfathers and 'apostle' spoons. The link being - old men with beards.
Bandied about	Rumours, scandal, and gossip, popularised and spread by word of mouth.
Bang on	Right on target, accurate, bull's eye.
Bank on it	You can rely on it, a certainty, 'Don't bank on it' has the opposite meaning.
Barge pole	e.g. don't touch it with a barge pole, have nothing to do with it, keep it at a safe distance.

Barking up the wrong tree	Getting it wrong, and continuing to do so, getting the wrong end of the stick.
Bathers	Your swimming things, e.g. don't forget your bathers, also referred to as trunks for boys.
Batten down the hatches	Prepare for stormy weather, and not only at sea!
Batting along	Speeding along in a vehicle of any description.
Beam ends	Destitute, down on your luck, e.g. 'stony broke' and on your 'beam ends', at your 'wits end', or the sides of a ship at its greatest width.
BEANOS	Parties and jollifications with food, nosh ups, and bean feasts.
BEING AS REGULAR AS CLOCKWORK	Meant being reliable, punctual, something to aspire to, and including personal functions (an edict from Father).
Beat about the bush	Not coming to the point, never reaching a conclusion nor making a decision.
Beat up	Attack, demolish, injure or punish an adversary by force, or deliberately fly very low.
Beavering away	Industriously pursuing the completion of a task.
Bedlam	Mayhem, chaos, acting like lunatics, a hullabaloo.
Bee in your bonnet	A bright idea buzzing around in your head, or can be pleased with yourself, cock a hoop.
Being in a paddy	Being in a temper, being in a strop, stroppy.
Belch	Break wind from the throat.
BELL BOTTOMS	Wide bottom trousers without turn-ups ('flares' to you) as worn by sailors in the Royal Navy.
Belly full	Had enough, enough is enough, up to here with it, over fed, stuffed with food, and anything else come to that.
Belt up	A way of saying shut up emphatically.
Berk	A twit, a monumental twit, e.g. he was a 'right berk'.
Bet your bottom Dollar	Put all your money on what you believe to be a certainty, belief in a 'cert'.
Bewitched, bothered and bewildered	A popular song that caught on in the dance-halls.

BICKER	Whinge argumentatively, argue incessantly over minor matters.
Big wig	A very important person, a VIP, a big fish, a nob.
Billet	An evacuee's home.
Bind	A nuisance, an arduous and unpleasant thing that has to be done, e.g. 'much binding in the marsh' in wartime.
Bite or hit the dust	Cease to exist, unsuccessful, died, e.g. another one of his hare-brained schemes hit the dust.
Bitter end	The end of something unpleasant or an arduous conclusion, e.g. 'to the bitter end', and 'seeing it through to the bitter end'.
BLABBERMOUTH	Someone who 'blabbers,' who cannot keep secrets, and is prone to talking when they should have kept quiet.
Black or bad books	Being in someone's bad books means whatever you have done wrong has been remembered, noted and recorded.
Black list	How and where the names of wrongdoers are recorded.
Bleary eyed	Red eyed, weary and looking the worse for wear.
BLESS 'IS LITTLE COTTON SOCKS	Said in admiration of a new born babe, or young child.
Bless their little Mary	Bless their little tummy and bless their little appetite.
BLIGHTER	Untrustworthy person, eg. the blighter got away with it, a swindler, or trickster, someone bad at paying bills.
Blighty	A WW1 name for England that is still remembered, the song 'Take me back to dear old Blighty' has a special meaning for 'oldies'.
Blood thicker than water	Having a greater loyalty towards relatives than non-relatives.
Bloke or bloggs	Referring to a man whose name you do not know.
Blotting out	Erasing, obliterating, obscuring something from being seen, e.g. the past, truth or the Sun.
Blotting paper	Sheets of absorbent paper used to dry wet ink and prevent smudging.
BLOTTING YOUR COPY BOOK	The worst possible thing you could do at school, or for any wrong doing at any other time, come to that.

Blotto	Blind drunk, unconscious, or in a deep sleep.
Blow me down	Taken by or expressing surprise, 'would you believe it', *'Well I'm Blowed'*, Wow!
Blow off steam	Blow your top, vent your feelings, a way of dispersing pent-up anger.
Blow the gaff	Disclose a secret, betray a confidence, spill the beans.
Blurb	Instructions or information to be given or read before proceeding.
Bob	A shilling in old money, ten bob = ten shillings = four half-crowns.
Bobbed	A fashionable haircut for ladies, cut very short and rounded at the back.
Bob's your uncle	That's right, affirmative, ok I'll do it.
Bobby Shafto	*'Went to sea'* - the sea shanty.
Boffins	Government 'back-room boys' engaged upon secret wartime inventions, e.g. radar.
BOG	Lavatory, lav, lavvy, loo, latrine, khazi, toilet.
Bold as brass	Knows no fear, goes where Angels may fear to tread.
Bone idle	Lazy in the extreme.
BONE IN HER MOUTH	The bow wave of a ship underway, revealing her speed through the water.
Bone to pick	Seek or have an argument or dispute with someone.
Bonkers	Crazy, mad, as in 'stark raving bonkers'.
Boogie woogie	A popular dance-hall craze brought over from America.
Bootstraps	To 'pull yourself up by your bootstraps', is to recover by redoubling your efforts, and/or by trying harder.
Bottom drawer	A special drawer reserved by a young lady for her trousseau, and clothes for special days. See top drawer.
Bottle	Courage, spunk, fearless.
Bottoms up	Chin chin, down with the drink, or down the hatch.
BOUNDER	Thoroughly untrustworthy, a man with a dodgy reputation, e.g. a bad payer.

Bowing and scraping	Being servile, condescending, curry favour, ingratiate oneself.
Brass monkeys	Cold in the extreme, see also shrammed.
Brass tacks	Get down to business, the fine detail, or nitty-gritty.
BREAD AND PULL(ET) IT	Said as a joke in wartime when making scarce food go further.
Bringing home the bacon	Coming back with something special, e.g. a treat in wartime.
British restaurant	A place to eat in wartime without coupons, and open to everyone.
BUGGINS	'Mrs Buggins', used when you cannot remember the name of a person you are referring to, e.g. you know, Mrs. Buggins. See Cadigans.
Bully beef	Tinned corned beef, or salt beef.
Bunking off	Disappearing, playing truant, i.e. bunking off school, 'swanning' off, or to 'skive' off.
BURNING YOUR BOATS	Doing something from which you cannot escape. To entrap oneself. Cutting off your only means of escape or return. e.g. leaving home under duress.
Busting your boiler	Exceeding your physical limits, doing yourself harm, dying for a pee.
Butterfingers	Clumsy, let slip through your fingers, fumbling a catch.
BUTTER WOULDN'T MELT IN 'IS MOUTH	As good as gold, endowing a sublime goodness upon an infant, or can be used sarcastically, e.g. he/she can do no wrong.
By and by	Later on, sometime in the future, e.g. 'it *may* happen by and by'.
By and large	More or less true, all things considered about right.
By hook or by crook	Somehow we'll manage to do it, the determination to succeed.
By the by	Incidentally, a passing thought, now I come to think of it, now it comes to mind.
By the skin of your teeth	'Missing it by the skin of your teeth'. A narrow miss, a narrow escape, or succeeding only by a very narrow margin, e.g. just scraping through.

'Chish and Fips'

Caboodle	A contraption made up of bits, a miss-mash, mix-up, the whole lot, e.g. 'the whole caboodle was a shambles'.
Caboose	A small shed or hut or a Guards van on American Railroads.
CACKHANDED	Awkward, not practical, always making a mess of things.
Canned	Drunk.
Cantankerous	Obstreperous, perverse, deliberately awkward, tetchy naughty and contrary.
Caps	Caps: school, thinking, dunce's, and percussion.
Cap covers *on*	From May to October sailors were required to wear immaculately 'blancoed' white cap covers.
Carry the can	Responsible and blamed when things go wrong.
CATNAP	A short sleep, doze or snooze, a little shut eye.
Cat o' nine tails	A flail inflicting severe wounds on the back as a punishment by flogging.
Cats and dogs	Heavy rain, stair rods, tipping it down.
Cat's whisker	A narrow gap or near miss, e.g. 'we only missed a collision by a cat's whisker', also a part of an early wireless set.
Caught by the scruff of the neck	Well and truly captured, restrained, or apprehended.
Caught napping	Caught unawares, caught unexpectedly, caught snoozing.
Caught on	A new idea, trend or fashion that became popular.
Caught out	Found out, rumbled, by trapping the offender.
CAUGHT SHORT	A dash to the loo.
Chancer	One who lives by taking risks.
CHAMFER UP	Make a poor job look better, or make a good job look even better, according to the woodwork master.

Chara/Charabanc	An omnibus used for 'outings' and 'rides' usually a single-decker and open-topped.
Cheek by jowl	Bit by bit, piece by piece, step by step, side by side.
CHERRY STICKS	Devices mounted on the front mudguards of motorcars to assist in judging the distance from the kerb. Posh ones lit up.
Chin chin	Said before having a friendly drink, which Father would follow by saying 'down with the drink' (did this mean he was for or against?)
Chinwag	To have a good old chat.
CHISH AND FIPS	Fish and chips.
CHOCKER	Fed up, had it up to here, cheesed off, fed up to the back teeth.
Chocker block	Full up, over full, full to the brim, stuffed.
Chocolate mud	Stodgy chocolate semolina pudding, often referred to as Gosport mud.
Chopsing	Chatting, gossiping.
Civvy Street	The place most servicemen and women wished to return to after getting 'demobbed'.
CLAMMY	Referring to the weather or the skin to touch when they are unpleasantly moist and cold.
Clapped out	Worn out, exhausted, beyond repair, only good for the scrap heap.
Claptrap	Verbal nonsense, words of little or no significance.
Clear as mud	Unclear, not understood, far from being clear.
Clear the decks	Tidy up, make ready, start afresh, prepare for a change.
Clever clogs	An above average person, cleverer than most. A bit of a know all, a smart Alec, sometimes used in a slightly derogative way.
CLEM SOHN	see The Bird Man.
Clink	Prison, jankers, jail, the cooler, and the nick.
Clobber	Assorted clothes for various purposes, e.g. country clobber. also to clobber someone is to knock 'em out, hit them hard, lay 'em flat.

Clot	Someone who does silly or stupid things, and breaks things easily e.g. a clumsy clot.
Cobblers	Talking rubbish, nonsense, untrue, unbelievable.
Cock, cocker	A basic form of addressing a man, e.g. how do my old 'cock' or my old 'cocker'.
Cock and bull	e.g. 'a cock and bull yarn', is not to be believed, to be taken with a pinch of salt, not to be taken as gospel.
Cock a hoop	Overjoyed, over the moon, extremely pleased.
Cocked dice	A faulty and invalid throw of the dice, not ending up flat on the table or board.
Cockeyed	A squint in the eye, and more generally not quite straight, out of true, skew whiff.
Cock shy	Throwing an object at a fairground target, or to have a go at hitting something.
Cock sure	Certain without a doubt, but may turn out to be wrong, overconfident.
Cock up	To cock something up is to ruin it. To bring about a major disaster is to make a 'monumental' cock up.
Cocky	Stuck up, over confident, a know-all.
Codswallop	Talking rubbish, far from the truth, make-believe.
Coffin nails	Woodbine cigarettes.
Cold feet	Scared to do something, cry off, back out, back off, afraid to go through with it.
Cold cream	A famous soothing face cream known as 'Ponds Cold Cream', white cream in a little dark blue jar.
COLLYWOBBLES	Funny feelings in the tummy, can be a prelude to the 'runs' or 'trots'.
COOL, CALM AND COLLECTED	The way you always ought to be even when provoked, (according to Father).
Coo-ee	A call to reveal your presence, or used to attract someone's attention.
Come a cropper	End up having a mishap, an accident, a misfortune.
COME TO THAT	In the same sense, in the same way, as a further example.

Come up trumps	Succeed, win, turn out right.
Commandeer	Compulsorily acquire for military purposes.
Commonorgarden	Ordinary, everyday, nothing special, nondescript.
CONFLAB	A group discussion, family conference, everyone going into a huddle.
Copy book	A school exercise book of model writing usually in thick and thin which had to be painstakingly copied.
Copper(s)	A penny (pennies) in old money, e.g. 'Can you spare a copper or two'.
Copper bottomed	A watertight, safe, secure, and long lasting assurance, a guarantee.
Copper plate	A 'model', and example of good handwriting, an example to follow or copy, a benchmark for excellence.
Cor luv a duck, Crikey, and Cor blimey	Expressions of surprise, or incredulity, e.g. 'for crying out loud'.
COUPONS	Were the means by which food, sweets, clothes, petrol and other essentials in short supply were rationed during the War.
CRAB FAT	Lubricating grease.
Cramp one's style	An attempt by an opponent to restrict or constrain one's actions, or performance.
Crank(y)	Round the bend, do stupid or crazy things, or to wind-up (crank) a car engine, hence crank-handle.
Crash bang wallop	Said when describing one or more extremely loud noises.
Craven A	Cigarettes with the claim - 'will not affect the throat'.
Crooning	A popular form of singing in a slow and sentimental way, e.g. Bing Crosby.
Crossed knives	Seeing them is unlucky according to superstition.
Crow's nest	A place high up the mast from which a good lookout should be kept.
Crummy	Dirty, unsavoury, down at heel, disreputable.
CRUMPET OR CRACKLING	Attractive young ladies, e.g. 'she's a lovely bit of crackling'.

Cupboard love	Love only given as a means of getting something in return, e.g. a child craving a toy.
Curios	Bric-a-brac, collectables, curiosities, unusual items.
Curtains	It's finished, its over, it stops right here, referring to almost anything.
Cushy	An easy job or task, hence, 'a cushy little number'.
Cut the cackle	An instruction to stop, curtail or reduce the talking.
Cut to the quick	Deeply and emotionally hurt, traumatised, slighted.

'Doollaly'

DAB HAND	Expert and adept at doing something, or anything come to that.
Damsel in distress	A young lady in a spot of bother, or in danger (is there a male equivalent?)
Dandy	An elaborately overdressed man, a fop. Also the name of a weekly comic.
Davy Jones's locker	Your destination when drowned at sea.
Dawdle	Move and walk slowly to no particular purpose, with time to spare, meander.
DECOKE	An essential procedure carried out when the car was 'laid up' in winter to improve the performance of its side valve engine ready for next Spring.
De da, de da	And so on and so on, ad infinitum, often said in mockery.
DEKKO	Take a look, have a look, have a shufti, peruse.
De Reske Minors	Father's favourite fags.
Deuce of a	A way of emphasising the size or extent of an extraordinarily difficult problem, or situation.
Dibs	The game of five stones e.g. ones-ees, twos-ees etc. Marble arch, towers, castles, spider's web and bunny in the hole.
Dicky	Not feeling so good, unwell, off colour, e.g. to have a dicky ticker was to have a bad heart or palpitations.
Dicky seat	An extra seat that could be opened up at the back of an 'open' car.
Diddems	A way of mocking anyone of any age when they act childishly, e.g. a response to crocodile tears.
Diddycoy	Gypsy, itinerant tinker.

Digs and Diggers	What we called our homes and new Mums when evacuated.
Dilettante	Someone who has ability and outstanding talents but fails to use them, a lazy bones, a backslider, a dabbler, a trifler.
Dilly dally	Dawdle, loiter, to be a slow coach, shilly shally.
Dimples	Natural dents in the cheeks or chin, having them went in and out of feminine fashion with Shirley Temple and other film stars'.
Dimwit	Not very bright at school, a dunce or duffer.
Dinlo	A fool, not a very bright person, not the full shilling.
Ditch	Land a crippled aircraft on the sea, or for a pilot to bale-out over water, or can mean to drop or discontinue an arrangement, e.g. he's 'ditched' me!.
Divi	Dividend, e.g. the Co-op Divi, a forerunner of cashback.
Do a Bunk	Disappear off the face of the earth, e.g. when bankrupt.
Dobying	A term used in the services for washing clothes.
DOCKYARD MATEY	The name given to employees in the Royal Naval Dockyard Portsmouth.
DOCTOR'S ORDERS	An instruction issued as though it was with the authority of a doctor, with the purpose of ensuring it is carried out.
Doddle	Easily done, easy to do, e.g. doing it was a doddle.
Dodging the column	Not pulling your weight, not doing your bit, avoiding your part in teamwork.
Dodgy	Suspect, unreliable, risky, e.g. poor workmanship.
Doggo	Staying put, lying low, not attracting attention.
Dog's body	Someone who is at everyone's beck and call.
Dog eared	Turned up at the corners, and looking the worse for wear.
Dog house	To be in the 'dog house' is to be male and in trouble from a female. Is there such a thing as a 'cat house'?
DOLLOP	A large spoonful of food casually dropped onto a plate without finesse.
Done and dusted	Completely finished in all respects.
Done for	Expired, died, finished off, dead, dying or about to do so.

Done in	Exhausted, extremely fatigued, at the end of your tether, had enough, fit for nothing.
Done thing	Conforming to what is socially acceptable, doing the proper thing.
Done to a turn or 't'	Said as a compliment to perfect baking.
DONKEYS' YEARS AGO	Referring to a very long time ago, ages ago, in the dim and distant.
Don't get your hackles up	"Don't get uppity with me", and advice not be provoked into getting annoyed or railed.
Don't touch it with a bargepole	Have nothing to do with it, give it a wide berth, keep well away, keep it at a distance.
Doo daa	See Cadigans.
DOOLALLY	Mad, crazy, round the twist, round the bend, 'mental'.
DOORSTEPS	Thick slices of bread and butter.
Dose of salts	E.g. going through like a 'dose of salts' refers to a process that is without problems and progressing quickly, a laxative perhaps?
Dosh	Money, aka lolly.
Double Dutch	Words without meaning, or understanding.
Down the	Usually means going south.
Down the lake (Let's go)	To sail our model yachts on the Canoe Lake, Southsea.
Down the garden path	To be taken on a path that leads nowhere, a false trail, (see 'up the garden path').
DOWN THE HARD OR DOWN THE FERRY	Implies that you then cross the harbour by Gosport ferry to Portsmouth.
Down the line	Sending a message by telephone, 'wire', or tele-printer.
Down the pond (Let's go)	To sail model boats in the pond in Walpole Park, Gosport. i.e. going south from Grove Road.
Doubting Thomas	Someone who is always unsure, and reluctant to agree with or to anything.
DRAIN PIPES	Macaroni, the only pasta we had that was not in a tin or in tomato sauce. Not forgetting tight legged trousers.

Dreadnought	Dread nothing, Royal Naval battleships armed with superior firepower (first one launched in 1906).
Dregs	What's left after the best has gone, e.g. tea leaves left in the bottom of the cup, and the dregs of society.
DRESSED UP TO THE NINES	Wearing your 'best' but not always the most appropriate clothes, a comment upon being overdressed for the occasion, or even said out of jealousy.
Dressing down	Being told off by someone in authority or of a higher rank.
Dribs and drabs	Things arriving in bits and pieces, bit by bit, little by little.
Droke or drokeway	An alleyway, a passageway.
Drip	Someone not quite up to it, limp, a bit of a 'drip', a 'wet week'.
Drum up	Canvas, rally, goad support, or drum up sufficient courage and determination.
Drumming it into someone	Forcing the point home which may take time and effort.
Drummed out	Thrown out in disgrace.
Duberry	'Duberry' is a word used as a substitute for something you cannot remember the name of (see Cadigans).
Duffer	Someone not very bright at school, a dunce, a dimwit.
Dull as ditchwater	A person without a spark of life, dull in the extreme.
Dunce's cap	A white conical hat with a big D on it, placed upon the head of a not so bright pupil in class, as a punishment for being 'dim'.
DV or dv	Hopefully, or with God willing and a fair wind we'll get there, fingers crossed.

'Ee needs a dose of thinners'

Earwigging	A method used to influence or persuade someone, e.g. lobbying.
Easy peasy	Take your time, take it easy, slow down.
Eee by gum	A northern way of expressing surprise, and incredulity, popularised by comedians of the day.
EE CUPS	Involuntary spasms of vocalised indigestion, an attack of the 'burps'.
Eeking it out	Making a little go a long way, e.g. bread and pull it.
EE NEEDS A DOSE OF THINNERS	The antidote to an over exuberant loudmouth.
Ee's in 'is element	A 'happy chappie', 'happy as Larry', he's enjoying himself, contented, doing what he likes doing.
EFFELLANT	Child speak for elephant (no not effluent).
Egg on	Encourage, chivvy, cheer on, connive in making someone do something.
EKCOs	Popular bakelite radios, some with circular cabinets and sunrise motifs.
ESKIMO NELL	Who in our youth had many a 'tale' written and sung about her exploits, but not heard of recently.
Even stevens	Equal score, a draw, evenly matched, level playing-field.
EVERSO	Exceedingly so, eg. thanks everso, ta everso.
EVERY PICTURE TELLS A STORY	Exactly what it says, sometimes used to emphasize an ache or pain, and other shortcomings felt in old age.
EVERYTHING IN THE GARDEN IS LUV'ERLY	A way of saying everything's fine and dandy, at least for the time being, or masking the fact that it is not, being optimistic.
Eyes like organ stops or chapel hat pegs	Protruding eyes, 'eyes sticking out on stalks'. A classic sign of thyrotoxicosis.

'Flummoxed'

Face ache	Someone who is a pain, as in he or she is 'a pain in the neck' and in many other places.
Face lift	Facial improvement by cosmetic surgery, then later used to describe improving any exterior, currently called a make-over.
Fag	A cigarette, or 'it's a fag' meaning something you don't like doing, its tiring, e.g. becoming fagged out.
Fair enough	OK! that's acceptable, agreeing or conceding to an alternative suggestion, or a compromise.
Farewell jetty	The South Railway Jetty in Portsmouth Dockyard used for important Naval arrivals and departures.
Fashion plate	Glamour 'Puss', or Glamour girl. See also 'Plates'.
FATHOM IT OUT	Solving a mystery, puzzle or problem by plumbing the depths of one's knowledge.
FFI	Free from infection, a medical all-clear as given in the Services.
FIBS	Little white lies, porkies, half-truths, e.g. telling fibs.
Fidget, fidgety phil	Can't keep still, has a touch of St.Vitus' dance.
Fiddle	Achieve by deceit, fraud or swindle, e.g. fiddle the books.
Fiddlesticks	A contradiction over accuracy, or truth, denouncing something as nonsense.
Fifty fifty	Someone who is only half with it, or only half there or has one half missing.
Fine and dandy	Everything is OK, just fine, couldn't be better.
Fine fettle	In excellent condition, fit for anything.
FINGIES AND FINGIES CROSSED	Fingers crossed, a sign indicating hope rather than certainty e.g. the lottery logo, or a sign of giving up, or wanting a truce 'pax' in a game.

Fire watching	A misnomer. A wartime term for spotting and putting out fires caused by incendiary or H.E. bombs.
Fishy	Suspect, suspicious, dodgy, e.g. it smells fishy.
Five stones	A hand game, see also Dibs.
Flake out	Lose consciousness, collapse.
FLAKED OUT	Collapsed, fainted, feeling exhausted.
FLANNEL	As in 'soft soap', a ploy to achieve something by beguile and flattery. Also a hardwearing material made into clothes that itched.
Flapjack	A face powder compact.
Flash lamp/light	A hand torch or bicycle lamp, see also Acetylene.
Flibbertigibbet	Mischievous, and Puck like, usually referring to a female.
Flicks	The 'pictures', cinema, the 'movies' e.g. from the flickering images of early films, hence going to the 'flicks'.
FLIM FLAM	Lightly disguised guile or mild deception.
Flippertygibbet	A scatty young girl, carefree and winsome. See 'Flibberti'.
FLIVVER	Affectionate name given to a small family car, e.g. an Austin 7, or Morris Minor.
Flog a dead horse	Effort to no avail, persist in trying when there is no chance of achieving the goal.
Florin	Two shillings, or two bob in old money.
FLUENCE	Exerting power, pressure or persuasion, hence 'putting on the fluence'. Fluence was sometimes the word used for electricity or power.
FLUFF	A nice little bit of 'fluff', said of a very attractive young lady.
FLUKE, FLUKY	Happened by accident, or by chance, or was unpredicted e.g. a fluky wind, one that keeps on changing direction.
FLUMMOXED	Confused, non-plussed, bewildered, flustered, outwitted and speechless.
Fly a kite	Float an idea, make a proposal.
Flying flossies	Dummies used in testing catapults for Naval Aircraft.

FOR CRYING OUT LOUD	A plea or an expression of extreme exasperation, said when under severe provocation.
Forking out	Paying through the nose for something you could ill afford, buying something you thought was expensive.
Forsythe, Seaman and Farrell	An often mimicked popular music hall act.
For the high jump	In dead, deep, real or serious trouble.
FORTY WINKS	Have a short snooze, take a brief sleep between duties or watches, have a nap or kip.
Foxed	Non-plussed, baffled.
FRED KARNO'S ARMY	A motley crew, an unruly bunch, an example of how not to run an army or any organisation come to that.
Freeman, Hardy and Willis	A popular 'high street' shoe-shop.
FROG'S SPAWN	Sago pudding.
Fudge	More or less reach the right outcome or result by dodgy, doubtful or unreliable means.
Fuddy duddy	A stick in the mud, a fuss pot, a silly or fussy person.
Fume	Extremely cross, irate, incandescent with rage, outraged, spitting blood.
Full steam ahead	Go as fast as you can.

G

'Gift of the gab'

Gabble	Talk too quickly.
Gaff	A faux pas, a social indiscretion, also part of the rigging of a sailing ship.
GALANTINE	A popular, cheap cold meat used sliced in rolls and sandwiches, e.g. like brawn.
Gallivanting and Gadding about	Going out and having a great time.
Galore	Plentiful, in abundance, e.g. 'whisky galore'.
GALOSHES	Shiny black overshoes or slip-overs used in wet weather, very popular and fashionable with the well-dressed to protect their expensive leather shoes.
Gash	Spare, superfluous, unwanted, government surplus, any waste material.
Gas mantle	A delicate structure that burned to produce the light of a gas lamp.
Gavorting	A way of gallivanting and gadding about. e.g, gavorting about on the dance floor.
Gawd's strewth, or just strewth on its own	Swearing the truth, expressing disbelief, surprise, or incredulity.
Geezer	An old geezer, an elderly upper class gent, a 'Colonel Blimp'.
Gee wizz	Exclamation of glee, incredulity, surprise or amazement.
Gently Bentley	Slow down, easy does it.
Gert and Daisy	Elsie and Doris Walters, sisters of Jack Warner.
Get cracking	The order to start, get a move on, or to speed up.
Get shot of	Dispose of, get rid of, with glee, delight, or relief.

Getting a green rub	To be unfairly treated, not deserving the treatment meted out to you.
Getting along like a house on fire	A way of saying very good progress is being made, two people getting on well together, i.e. hitting it off.
Getting away with it	Not getting caught, a narrow scrape, a close shave.
Getting by or just about getting along	Just about surviving, and up against it.
Getting carried away	An obsession, taking things too far, borne along on a wave of euphoria.
Getting down to brass tacks	Reaching a meaningful discourse, discussing the nitty gritty, down to the fine detail.
Getting out of bed on the wrong side	Grumpy, awkward and bad tempered was said to be the result of having done so.
Getting someone's goat	Annoying someone in the extreme.
Getting the hang of it	Beginning to be able to do something, in the early stages of learning a new skill, or knack.
Getting the push	Getting the sack, getting fired, getting the heave ho.
Getting the wrong end of the stick	Completely misunderstanding, or misinterpreting the situation.
GETTING YOUR FEET UNDER THE TABLE	Usually means making every effort to get accepted by 'her' parents and family, 'getting well in' with them.
GET TO WINDWARD	Getting the better of someone, one upmanship.
Get your finger out	Get a move on, buck up, don't delay any longer.
GIFT OF THE GAB	The ability to speak at length and excessively, but not always appreciated, talking too much too often.
Git or gink	A queer or odd looking so and so, describing an 'oddball'.
GIVE 'EM SOCKS	Give them a good hiding, knock the stuffing out of them, give 'em what for.
Give 'em what for	Retaliate by giving them a bigger hiding, or more grief than they gave you.
Give me strength	Spontaneous response to encountering something exasperating, unexpected, hard to believe, or difficult to cope with.

Gives me the creeps	Unpleasant reaction to something spooky, producing a shiver down your spine.
GLAD RAGS	Your best clothes, Sunday best, wearing old clothes but the best you have got.
Gnat's pee	A weak cup of tea.
Go a bundle on	Like something very much.
Go cart	Homemade buggy, four pram wheels, axles and a plank of wood.
Going at it hammer and tongs	An all out effort, can refer to an argument, a fracas.
Going down the hard	To catch the Gosport ferry across to Pompey.
Going down the pond	To watch the International Model Yacht races or having rides in the paddle boats in Walpole Park Gosport.
Going down town or just saying 'going out'	Usually meant cycling down to Woolworths, near the Ferry Gardens, to meet the gang.
Going north over Portsdown Hill	Leaving roots and home for the great wide world that is just over the hill. (See 'burning your boats').
GOING OFF THE DEEP END	Getting up a temper, in a strop, stroppy, leading off, losing your temper.
GOING OUT THE FRONT	Said when going out to Stokes Bay or Southsea Beach, i.e. going out the bay, or going out the beach.
Going up	Going north.
Going down	Going south.
Going along or across	Going east or west. (See GRTH).
GOINGS ON	Happenings, a to do, things taking place that are not quite right or untoward.
Golden rivet	Delicate part of the male anatomy.
Going to the 'Social'	Going to the local 'hop', dancing to gramophone records, and a revolving mirror-ball, ending wih a smoochy last waltz.
GOLLY	Short for Golliwog, a black faced doll which became a craze and a favourite in most children's homes, Debussy even composed a 'Golliwog's cake-walk', the use of 'Golliwog' is no longer politically correct.

Golliwog badges	A great favourite with children, issued in pots of Robertson's marmalade and jams, and pinned to our lapels next to other collectibles such as the Ovaltinies badge.
Golly Gosh and Golly Gumdrops	Expressions of surprise.
Gone bust	Lost all your money, bankrupt.
Gone for a burton	Come a cropper, had an accident and disappeared off the face of the earth.
Goner	Dead, departed, as in he's a 'goner', or just disappeared without trace.
GONE DOWN THE PAN	Something lost or wasted, a failed enterprise, only fit for disposal, no longer used, best flushed 'dtp'.
Gone to pot	Deteriorated, gone to rack and ruin, beyond repair.
Gone west	Disappeared into the sunset, lost without trace.
Good as gold	Praise or exaggeration of a child being well behaved.
Go to pot	Equivalent to saying 'Go to hell for all I care', or wishing someone elsewhere, or to have a sticky end.
GOODNIGHT LISTENERS EVERYWHERE	Said at the end of BBC Home Service radio transmissions for the day, and said by a posh southern voiced announcer.
Good night, sleep tight, hope the bugs don't bite	Said with affection to children at bedtime.
GOSPORT	aka Turktown, God's Port, Gorse Port, or Go-sport.
Got any gum chum	Catch phrase said when cadging Wrigley's chewing gum from American servicemen, or Nylons, or Camels or Chesterfields, come to that.
Gotcha!	Caught you!, caught you out, you're trapped.
Grapevine	Bush telegraph, reliable and alternative sources for the communication of information.
Great gusto	Maximum effort, putting everything you've got into it, doing it with enthusiasm.
Great scott	Expressing surprise at the unexpected.

Gremlins	Little 'fellers' that had a habit of ruining things, i.e. often putting a spanner in the works.
Gripe	Complain, moan and groan, whinge, hence gripe water for fractious babies.
Grog	Navy rum.
GROG BLOSSOM	Red Faced, flushed cheeks from drinking the grog.
Groggy	Feeling unwell, under the weather, looking the worse for wear from a hangover.
Grot	Something unpleasant to eat, e.g. pink grot, for pink blancmange.
Grotty	As groggy, also uncared for, dirty, grubby, or in a poor state of repair, also feeling unwell, under the weather.
GRTH	Going Round The Hill (Portsdown Hill) by road. From Gosport up to Fareham, along to Portchester, and Cosham, then down into Pompey rather than crossing the Harbour by ferry boat or by floating-bridge.
Grubby	Dirty, unclean, could do with a wash.
Guffaw	A coarse or boisterous laugh, sometimes used as comment upon authenticity or authority.
Guzzle	Drink noisily and with great gusto.
Guv'nor	A more familiar form of address than sir, short for governor.
GYP	Acute pain, it gives me 'gyp'.

'Hoppin' out at Fratton' (stn)

Half cut	Drunk.
Half hitch	Pinch, steal, acquire.
Hamfisted	Awkward, lacking in dexterity, all fingers and thumbs, not practical.
Hand to mouth	A precarious existence not knowing where your next meal is coming from.
Hankies	To blow your nose on. A cellophane box of 'Pyramid' linen hankies were popular Christmas presents.
Harbour a grouse	Have a long-standing chip on your shoulder, to bear a grudge.
Hard and fast	e.g. a hard and fast rule, one which cannot be changed, immutable, also a ship well and truly stuck on a rock at low tide.
HARD CHEESE or hard cheddar	Said to someone when they have hard or bad luck.
Hard up	Not much money, no money to spare, broke, penniless.
HARDWAY	At the top of Grove Road, an embarkation point for D-Day.
Hare-brained	A person who is scatty, always thinking up mad schemes, or having crazy ideas.
Have no truck with it	Have absolutely nothing to do with it.
Haven't got the foggiest	Haven't got a clue, don't know.
Having a finger in the pie	Getting involved in something, and not always being welcome.
Having a screw loose	Not all there, crazy, lacking that certain something.
Haywire	All messed up, disarray, disorganised, gone to pot.
HEADING NORTH OVER PORTSDOWN HILL	Leaving home to explore the great wide world beyond. aka burning your boats.

Head over heels	Gone over the top, gone overboard, e.g. 'head over heels in love'.
Heart throb	Sweetheart, someone you loved passionately when young but maybe only for a short time before someone else came along.
HELLZAPOPPIN	The memorable title of a wacky, zany 1941 film, can't remember much about it, but I can remember what 'Louisiana Purchase' was all about.
Hiatus	A rumpus, argument or dispute.
Hifulutin	Superficial, frippery, of little consequence, so much hot air, pseudo superior.
Higgledy piggledy	An untidy mess, topsy-turvy. All over the place, in no particular order.
Highbrow	An indicator and label of sophisticated cultural taste and preference, e.g. classical music before the days of Classic FM.
High and dry	A difficult situation from which there is little chance of immediate escape, stranded well above the high water mark.
High as a kite	Drunk, inebriated, squiffy.
Highly strung	Taut, temperamental, nervy, tense, always on edge, rarely relaxed.
Highups	Bosses, often referred to as 'them what's in charge'.
His Nibbs	A person of some standing, importance, or affection, the boss.
HIT THE DECK	Fall to the ground, a hard fall, crash land on an aircraft carrier, or anywhere come to that.
Hoighty toity	Stuck up, haughty, petulant.
Hokey cokey	A popular dance at 'hops'.
HOLD THE FORT	The responsibility for looking after, and the safe keeping of a building or property, in someone's absence.
Hook, line and sinker	Everything, the lot, the complete works, not forgetting anything.
Hop	Popular name for a 'social' or local dance.

HOPPIN' OUT AT FRATTON (Stn)	Refers to sailors who have for years regularly evaded paying the full rail fare from Waterloo; for the other meaning you'll have to ask a sailor, or his girl friend!
Hopscotch	A perennial girl's game, played anywhere you can chalk numbered squares.
Horny	A male feeling sexy.
Hostilities	Another name for being at war.
Hotchpotch	A muddle, a mishmash, a kuddle-muddle, mix-up.
HOT WALLS	The name given to the sea defences approaching the mouth of the harbour on the Portsmouth side.
Hubbub	A clamour of voices, a din.
Huff or huffy	Being in a huff is to be in a temper, cross, stroppy.
Hullabaloo	An excess of noise and loud voices, a din, a schemozzle.
Humdinger	Outstanding, something really special, a real beauty.
Hundreds and thousands	Small sweets, a large number of which could be bought for a penny.
Hunkey dory	Everything is fine, just fine, fine and dandy.

'Is you is, or is you ain't my baby?'

If Bob's your Uncle then Fanny's my Aunt	A long-winded way of expressing disbelief.
I wouldn't put it past him/her	Expectations and suspicions, e.g. I wouldn't be a bit surprised if they changed their minds again.
If you can read the time by the clock on the Church in Ryde from Stokes Bay, *It is sure to rain, or it's just left off*	A local weather portent.
In summer if the wind is in the east, and you can hear the chimes of the Guildhall clock, you can be sure of a fine day	Another one.
In summer on a fine day if the wind comes up in the east and goes round with the sun you can sail a 12 foot dinghy from Stokes Bay all the way to Yarmouth I.O.W. and back within the day *- we did, Joyce and I!*	Something that may happen only once in a lifetime. (Subsequently revised to - *will* only happen once in our lifetime).
If your ears are burning	Somebody is talking about you, or taking your name in vain.
I haven't heard a dicky bird	Haven't heard a thing.
If you want to get ahead get a hat, and if you cannot fight wear a big hat	Two pieces of supposedly good advice often quoted by Father.
I'm all right Jack	The pursuit of self-interest.

In a jiff or jiffy	Done quickly, coming soon, won't take long.
In a pickle	In difficulty, in a mess, a spot of bother.
In a stew	All mixed up, confused, angry.
In one ear and out the other	Not listening, or incapable of remembering what is being said to you.
IN STOOK	In some sort of trouble, or in deep trouble.
IN A TIZZ-WOZZ	In a state of concern, confusion and turmoil.
In a tizzy	Ditto as above.
In a twinkling	Something that happens very quickly,.
In a two and eight	In a state of minor chaos, or in a tizzy as above.
Ink-well	A small removable china receptacle nesting in a hole in your school desk-top full of turgid often lumpy black ink. Cleaning out all the ink-wells was a school punishment.
In two shakes of a lamb's tail	What ever is to be done or happen, will be done or will happen quickly. Observe a lamb's tail and you'll get it!
IS YOU IS, OR IS YOU AIN'T MY BABY?	A catchy little number, and 'vocal' played and sung by dance bands and vocalists.
It's in the bag	We've got it, done it, its a certainty.
It's no skin off my nose	It makes no difference to me.
It was Bedlam	Noisy, and uncontrollable chaos, rowdy.
IT WON'T ACKLE	It won't or doesn't work.
I wouldn't put it past 'im	Unpredictable, unreliable, untrustworthy.
IZAL and Dettol	Father's favourite toiletries.

'Jolly Hockey Sticks'

Jack it in	End it, finish it, pack it in, give it up, call it a day.
Jalopy	A dilapidated old motor vehicle.
JANKERS	Sentenced to a term of imprisonment in the army.
JEEPERS CREEPERS	*'Where did you get those peepers'*, hit song, circa 1936, and a way of expressing surprise and/or admiration.
Jerk	Someone who has done something stupid, silly or inane.
JEW'S HARP	A small toy instrument, played with the mouth and both hands by blowing, sucking and twanging.
Jiggery pokery	Underhand behaviour, devious, deceitful, dishonest.
Jitterbug	Fast, energetic dance, popular at hops in the 40's.
Jitters	Scared, extremely nervous.
Joanna	Piano.
Joint	A place, shop or dwelling, e.g. It was a 'crummy joint', and as might be used today, a 'fast food' joint. Then there is the Sunday joint.
JOLLOP	Medicine (the sort you take not study).
JOLLY HOCKEY STICKS	Socially active and lively young ladies with an excess of enthusiasm for life and games, a Joyce Grenfell character certainly.
Jotting it down	Making notes for future reference, aide memoir.
JUICE	Electricity, petrol.
Just in the nick of time	Not a moment too soon, at the last possible moment, cutting it fine.
Just the job	Perfect, exactly what was wanted, just what the Doctor ordered.
Just what the doctor ordered	Exactly what was needed, just the job. Fits the bill precisely, meets all the requirements.

'A Kerfuffle'

KAZOO	A toy musical instrument which you blew or hummed into.
Keel over	Feint, collapse, fall down, a yacht dried out and on its beam ends.
Keep it under your hat	Keep it a secret, keep it to yourself, don't talk about it.
KEEPING AN EYE ON THE ENEMY	Watching the clock, having to watch the time.
Keep smiling through	A favourite wartime song popularised by Vera Lynn.
Keep your eyes peeled or skinned	Keep a sharp and constant lookout.
Keep your pecker up	Stay cheerful, and walk tall especially when things go wrong, also means eat well.
Keep your wig on	Keep your cool, be calm and collected, simmer down.
Kerfuffle or Kerfuddle	A monumental mix up, a complete mess, a fuss.
Kick the bucket	To die, peg out, expire.
Kinky	Not quite normal, querky, bent.
Kip	Sleep.
Kiss curl	A single large curl on either temple, sometimes as a part of a 'Marcel' wave.
Knack	To have a knack is to possess skill, talent, flair, and a bent.
Knee high to a grasshopper	A small person, a short arse, a nipper, titch, small fry.
Knick knacks	Bits and pieces, bric-a-brac, a collection of small favourite possessions.
Knocked for six	Confound, dumbfound, or defeat one's enemy or opponent. Sent packing or dismissed.
Knockers	Door to door tinkers.

KNOCK OFF	Pinch, steal, pilfer, also means to finish work at the end of the day, e.g. to 'knock off' at five thirty.
Knowing one's onions	e.g. 'he knew his onions' meant he knew a thing or two, was adept and well versed in his subject.
Knuckle down to it	Really get down to doing it, by making a supreme effort.

'Looking thru' two panes of glass'

Lackadaisical or lacksedaisical	Lazy, lazy bones, slipshod, idle, lacking oomph and drive, not caring two hoots.
La dee da	Acting 'Posh'.
Lady Muck	An ordinary woman acting 'Posh'.
LDB	Landport's Drapery Bazaar - a prominent, and much frequented departmental store in Commercial Road Portsmouth.
Lashing it down	Pouring with rain, coming down like stair rods, tipping it down, driving rain.
Lashings of	Plenty of, in abundance, e.g. hot water, luverly grub etc.
Launch	Ceremony for a ship entering the water for the first time. A small boat used for ferrying.
Leading light	'A leading light' is someone who sets an example, ahead of the crowd, outstanding in a special or certain way, one that others follow, also an important navigational aid.
LEAST SAID SOONEST MENDED	More Fatherly advice.
Legless	Drunk and incapable.
Leg it	Run for it, or walk instead of riding.
Let off steam	Blow your top, let it all out!, used as an escape valve.
Let the cat out of the bag	Revealing something that should have been kept a secret, blow the gaff.
Letting your hair down	Enjoying yourself, doing what you might not do normally.
LICK AND A PROMISE	An apology for a proper wash.
Like Billy o'	An indication of speed, haste, and emphasis e.g., 'he ran like billy o'.

Like it or lump it	Make your mind up one way or the other, Yes or No, say yes or go/do without.
LILLIPUT, HEALTH & EFFICIENCY, AND MEN ONLY	Undercover, 'educational mags', essential reading for schoolboys.
Limber up	Prepare to do something, exercise in preparation.
Limelight	'In the limelight' in the glare of publicity, exposed to the bright lights of fame.
LINGO	A language, dialect, as the locals speak, in the vernacular, e.g., learning the lingo.
Lippy	A profuse and avid talker, over chatty, having too much to say for themselves, bordering on being a bit of a 'madam', or 'pushy broad'.
Listening posts	Dotted along the coasts in wartime, an early means of detecting the approach of enemy bombers using dishes, microphones, and amplifiers.
LITTLE BLACK SAMBO	A much loved children's favourite, a black faced young boy, who featured in many books, stories and gramophone records.
Little tyke	Rascal, scallywag, e.g. you little tyke, or you little urchin.
Living in the lap of luxury	Affluent, someone said to be living in luxury, maybe said with a tinge of envy.
Load of old cobblers	Rubbish, nonsense, not to be believed, fairytales.
Lo and behold	'And it came to pass', there look at that, a revelation, e.g. a rabbit out of a hat, and would you believe it!
LOBBY LUDD	A character from a national newspaper, maybe the 'Daily Chronicle' seen at seaside promenades in summer who would give you ten 'bob' if you recognised him and said a special password.
Lockus	Chocolate.
Lock stock and barrel	Everything, the lot, the works, nothing left out.
Lolly	Money, aka dosh.
LONG WINDED	Slow to do anything, take ages to come to the point.
Looking pasty	Looking pale, wan and unwell.

LOOKING THRU' TWO PANES OF GLASS	Wearing spectacles.
Looney bin	A lunatic asylum, Bedlam, where all the loonies went.
LORD HAW HAW	An English traitor, William Joyce, who broadcast for the Germans. Eventually caught and executed as a traitor after the war.
Lucy Locket lost her pocket	Lucy lost her purse.
Lump it	Put up with it.
LUVERLY TELL YER MUM	A way of saying a big thank you.

'Mutton dressed as lamb'

Making a hash of it   Making an almighty mess of things.

Making a meal of it   Taking longer than necessary, deliberately going slow.

Making ends meet   Struggling financially to maintain a required standard of living, having to scrimp and save, and having to make sacrifices.

MAKING HEAVY WEATHER OF IT   Finding it difficult, up against it, making slow progress.

MALARKEY   Playing up, being awkward, humbug, nonsense, e.g. we'll soon put a stop to his malarkey.

Mangle   See an ACME and Wringer.

Me old cock
Me old cock robin   A particularly familiar way of addressing an old friend or acquaintance.

Minding one's P's and Q's   Being careful, do the right thing.

Mishmash   A mix-up, muddle, hotchpotch.

MOGGY   A nondescript cat.

Mooch about   Going about aimlessly, or without a lot of purpose, just waiting for something to happen, waiting at the lamppost at the corner of the street.

Money for old rope   Getting good money for something that is worthless, and getting good pay for doing very little.

Month of Sundays   Taking what seems to be an interminable length of time.

MOTH BALLS   An effective and necessary deterrent to stop moths eating holes in woollen clothes, but gave the clothes and those that wore them a pungent and unpleasant smell of camphor, you takes your choice.

MUDLARKS   Kids, boys as well as girls, recovering pennies thrown from the bridge by onlookers into deep black mud at Portsmouth Harbour Station.

MUM'S THE WORD   Keep quiet about it, 'be like dad keep mum', and 'careless talk costs lives,' popular wartime slogans.

MUSH   A none too complimentary way of a male addressing another male, e.g. 'Ere mush, what's your game?' and clear off 'mush'.

Mushy   Squashy, messy, runny, as in 'mushy peas'.

MUTTON DRESSED AS LAMB   A not so young woman dressed as though she was.

My Aunt Fanny   An expression emphasizing total disbelief.

My Giddy Aunt   An expression of surprise, reaction to, or excitement over the unexpected.

'Nincompoop'

NAAFI BOYS	Boys with No Aims, Ambition or Flippin' Interests (so what's new?)
NATIONAL BENZOLE	The fuel with 'oomph' we put in our cars and motorbikes.
Nail your colours to the mast	Reveal who or what you stand for, show which side you're on, fly your flag.
Namby pamby	A weak character, childish, a cry baby.
Nancy boy	Effeminate.
Neither rhyme nor reason	Without due cause, lacking in consideration, done without thinking.
New fangled	Describing new gadgetry.
Nifty	Smart, speedy, well suited, ideal for the job, e.g., 'a nifty bit of kit'.
Nigh	Nearly, almost, close to, coming up to, e.g., nigh six o' clock means it is nearly six o' clock.
NINCOMPOOP	A silly, stupid, incompetent person, a bit of a twit.
Nineteen to the dozen	Quickly, speedily, at a rate of knots.
Nine to five	Office Hours, always thought to be a 'cushy' little number.
Nipper	A small boy, 'the nipper' being the smallest of the family, also known as 'titch'.
Nitty Nora	The nurse who regularly visited school to eradicate infestations of the scalp.
No answer was the stern reply	A silent reprimand, a question met with a stony silence rather than an answer.
NOBS	The 'well to do', the 'upper crust', the nobility, the better off.
No can do	Decline a request, a refusal, say no.

North is up, south is down and east and west are across	So 'tis said.
Nosh	Food, hence the expression Nosh up, come and get it!
NOSMO KING	The name taken by a well known comedian from the No Smoking sign.
Not a dicky bird	Haven't said or heard a thing.
Not a jot	Couldn't care less, counts for nothing, nowt, nuffink.
NOT 'ARF	Emphatic agreement, or another way of saying yes please to something much desired.
Not one iota	Not even one tiny bit.
Nothing much up there	A disparaging remark about a person's apparent lack of brains, a 'dunce' or 'duffer'.
Not much cop	Not up to much, not worth the candle.
Not worth the candle	Not up to scratch, not worth the price, or the effort.
Nutter, nutcase	Erratic, does stupid and unexpected things, crazy, 'as nutty as a fruit cake'.

'On yer Bike'

Off 'is trolley	Unbalanced, with the balance of mind disturbed, a nut case.
OILSKINS	Wet weather gear for cyclists, cape, leggings and a sou'wester.
Old codger	Someone who is elderly and artful amongst men.
Old crocks	The frail and elderly, also old and well cared for motor cars.
Old salt	An old and experienced sailor.
ON A FIZZER	To be put on a charge, a form of army punishment.
On 'is last legs	Someone about to peg out, or not expected to be around much longer.
Once in a blue moon	A rare occurrence, seldom, hardly ever, not very often.
On edge	Nervous, jumpy, worrying about something and showing it, a bag of nerves.
One fell swoop	Completed in one clean and decisive action, over in one.
One over the eight	Drunk, having one drink too many.
One hand for the ship, and one for yourself	A reminder to take great care of yourself when carrying out a difficult job, e.g. 'up aloft' taking in sail.
On the level	Telling the truth, being honest, straight up, legit, reliable.
On the dot	Being punctual, a precise point in time, e.g. he always arrived on the dot of twelve.
On the sick list	Officially recognised, recorded, and known as unwell, and unfit for duty.
On the side of the angels	Someone who always gets it right, or always does the right thing is said to be 'siding with the angels'.
On the sunny side of the street	Choosing the brighter side of life and after all you only have to cross the street to find it.
ON THE TOP LINE	Ready to go, quick off the mark, on the fast track e.g. taking the upper platform at Portsmouth Town Station for the fast train to Waterloo, getting there in 90 minutes.

On tick	Paying later, i.e. before credit cards, and 'taking the waiting out of wanting'.
On with the motley	Let's get on with it no matter how bad it is, or what the outcome may be, a job or task that required a special effort.
ON YER BIKE	Push off, shove off, get lost, get going, and be off with you.
On yer bill	Being alone, doing it solo, 'go do it on your own'.
Oodles	Plenty, more than enough, a surplus.
Oojameeflick	You know - a 'thingamajig!' Made up words when you can't think of the proper one e.g. thingee, thingamabob. They are called Cadigans, (no not cardigans).
OOZELUM BIRD	A bird that flies round in ever decreasing circles.
Outings	Going out as a special treat e.g. a Charabanc ride, going 'tats', going somewhere nice.
Out of the blue	A complete and unexpected surprise, could be good or bad.
Out on your ear or neck	Thrown out, chucked out, get the sack, fired, dismissed.
Out the bay	Going out to Stokes Bay.
Ovaltineys	A children's club sponsored by the makers of the popular bed-time drink Ovaltine, famous for its badges and catchy jingle on Radio Luxembourg.
Over the hill	Past it, as in elderly, also inferred going over Portsdown Hill to see if there was a world that lay to the north.
Over the moon	Overjoyed, 'happy as Larry'.
OVER THE WATER	Crossing the Harbour by Ferry to Pompey, or vice-versa to Turktown. If you lived in Gosport then it was always called the Gosport Ferry in either direction.

'Pneumonia Bridge'

Pain in the proverbrial, neck or butt	A tiresome, irritating and unpopular person.
Palais glide	Another dance popular at 'hops' and 'socials'.
PALAVA, PALAVER	A fuss and bother made about very little, a fuss over nothing, something unnecessarily complicated and long winded.
PAPER DOLL	A 'fella's alternative to having a *'fickle minded real live girl'*, a lyric from a popular song of the day.
Parched	Thirsty.
Passion killers	Elasticated long legged knickers.
Pax	Peace, Pax as in PAXFORD. Saying pax and crossing your fingers would stop a fight, and you accepted defeat.
PEG OUT	Die, expire, collapse, kick the bucket. breathe your last, pass away, perish.
Penny dreadfuls	Sweets, comics, anything costing no more than a penny.
Penny's dropped	A belated understanding, the truth realised.
Percussion caps	Explosive devices on a long roll or individually in a 'pill box', as used in toy cap guns, or separately in toy bombs.
Pernickety	Over precise, unnecessarily fussy, extremely particular.
Phoney	Fake, false, two faced.
PHYSOG	Face, facial expression, countenance.
Pie eyed	Looking the worse for wear.
PIFFLE	Utter nonsense, talking rubbish, balderdash.
Pin ups	Pictures of 'Glamour Girls' pinned up on your wall. e.g. Jane Russell. (Never men in those days: that was yet to come).
Pip Squeak and Wilfred	Strip cartoon characters, also the name given to a group of three Royal Navy service medals.

Pipe your eye	Cry, shed a tear, blub.
Plates	Pictures, photographs and illustrations reproduced in books were called 'plates'.
Playing hooky	Bunking off school.
PLAY UP POMPEY	Chant of the Portsmouth Football Club Fans, sung to the chimes of the Guildhall Clock. (The same as Big Ben).
PLUS FOURS	A style of men's baggy trousers, gathered to just below the knee, like knickerbockers, were popular with golfers.
PNEUMONIA BRIDGE	A high windy bridge over Haslar Creek, notorious for catching 'chills' in wintertime.
POGS	Pinks Old Girls Society. (Mother was a POG).
POM POM	A Bofors multi-barrelled light anti-aircraft gun.
Ponds cold cream	A popular soothing skin cream applied before retiring, see cold cream.
POOL PETROL	The only brand of petrol available during the war, TVO was a much sought-after alternative.
Poppycock	Nonsense, rubbish, talking tosh, balderdash and piffle.
POSH	Wealthy, well to do, upper class, P.O.S.H., port side out, starboard home berths on board P&O liners was considered to be posh.
Pot calling kettle black	Criticising someone when you are just as bad, or even worse.
Praise the Lord and pass the ammunition	A popular war time song from the USA.
Prank	Practical joke, a mischief.
Press on	Keep going when the going is difficult or you're up against it, hence 'press on regardless'.
Prick your ears up	The reaction to hearing something of particular interest.
PROBLEMS	A common answer to the question, 'what did you do at school today?' was, 'we did problems'.
Prune	A foolish, daft, silly, stupid person.
PULHHEEMS	Known to most servicemen as the acronym for the basic medical examination. P - Physique, U - Upper limbs, L - Lower limbs, H - Hearing left ear, H - Hearing right ear, E - Eyes left, E - Eyes right, M - Mental capacity, S - Stamina.

Pulled up by your boot straps	Told to do better, or make an improvement.
Pull your horns in	Making savings, being less extravagant, economise.
Pull your socks up	Advice for you to improve and do much better.
Pull the other one or Pull the other leg	I don't believe you, you're kidding, stop kidding.
Pull the wool over your eyes	Prevent you from seeing the truth, hoodwink you into believing something other than the truth.
Punch	A long gone popular weekly magazine full of topical, political, cynical and humorous cartoons and articles. Sadly missed.
PUSH BIKE	The old name for a bicycle which required a big push on the pedals or with the foot on the ground to start off.
Push the boat out	Celebrate with no expense spared.
Pusser's	The Naval or seaman's word for Purser, meaning from the RN Stores, or something for or used by sailors, e.g., Pusser's Rum, Pusser's bread being a ship's loaf.
Pusser's duck	A Supermarine 'Walrus', a single-engined pusher amphibian of the Fleet Air Arm that frequented HMS Daedalus, Lee-on-Solent.
Put a sock in it	Don't say another word, shut up, shut it, belt up.
PUT BY	A sign in most wool shop windows, keeping wool of the same dye until you needed it, or could pay.
PUT THE KIBOSH OR MOCKERS ON IT	Finish it, put an end to it, squash it flat, stopped in its tracks.
Put or throw a spanner in the works	Ruin something, to bring something to a complete stop, put the mockers on it, kill it (the plan) stone dead.
Putting your foot in it	Doing something that you should not have done, making things worse, getting into a mess that's difficult to wriggle out of, messing things up.
Put upon	Make excessive and unreasonable demands, make someone a dogsbody.
Put up with it	Accept without complaint, lump it.

'I'm telling you this on the QT'

Queer one's pitch   An unfortunate action done in the past that prevents you from ever returning to the same place and be welcome, persona non grata.

Quid   A pound (£).

QUIDS IN   Pounds(£) better off, making a good financial deal, well in pocket.

QUINK   A posh brand of ink used in school, not favoured by teachers, Royal Blue was our favourite, had an addictive smell.

QT   On the quiet, secretly, in confidence, keep quiet about it, e.g. 'I'm telling you this on the QT'.

'Right as Rain'

Rack and Ruin	Deteriorated badly, gone to pot, dilapidated, ramshackle.
Ragamuffin	An untidy, unkempt, poorly dressed young urchin.
RAMSHACKLE	Untidy, in a poor state of repair, falling to bits, gone to rack and ruin.
Rascal	A scamp, a knave, a naughty boy, or a pet animal, can be used as a friendly reprimand as in "You little rascal".
Rhubarb rhubarb!	Mutterings of disbelief, and disagreement.
RIFF RAFF	So called 'rough' people, the opposite of being posh.
RIGHT AS RAIN	Being in good health, or back to rude health.
Rightho! or righty ho!	Cheerful agreement.
RIGMAROLE	A complicated, prolonged and often protracted procedure, sometimes pronounced riggermarole.
Rise and shine	An early wake up call.
Rotter	A nasty bit of work, always doing nasty things, despicable, a cheat.
Roughing it	Having a raw deal, enduring hardship, life in hard times.
Round and round the blackberry bush	Going round in circles, not getting to the point, prevaricate.
Round the bend or twist	Gone crazy, past it, left good sense behind, a nutter.
ROZZERS	Policemen, coppers, the fuzz.
RUBBED GREEN	Done down, unfairly treated, got the rough end of the stick.
Ruffian	A rough unkempt and aggressive male.
Rummage	Scrabbling through a collection of things, e.g. to rummage through a handbag, or jumble.
Run of the mill	Ordinary, routine, nothing special, nothing out of the ordinary.

'Stop me and buy one'

Saga	Something small to start with that turns into something big, something simple that ends up complicated and long drawn out, a long drawn out but otherwise enjoyable narrative or story.
Sarky	To make a sarcastic remark, to say something sarcastically.
Saucer'd and blow'd	The way to make the very hottest tea drinkable i.e. making the undrinkable drinkable.
Save our souls	SOS, the old international signal and Morse code for extreme distress at sea, superseded by 'mayday'.
SARSAPARILLA	A popular drink taken as a medicine to soothe irritation.
Scallywag	Same as Rascal, a scoundrel, a naughty, loveable young rogue, e.g. a pet dog or a child.
SCHEMOZZLE	A right old 'to do', a mighty mix-up, confusion.
Scram	An order to go, get lost, do a bunk, buzz off, scarper.
Scrapes	Getting into hot water, brushes with authority, or the law, avoiding trouble by the skin of your teeth.
SCARPER	Scram, move on, push off, get lost.
Scorcher	Heat wave.
SCREAMING ABDABS	A serious medical condition contracted in the 'services'.
Screwball	A crazy person, zany, erratic, unconventional.
Screw missing	One of the many ways to describe someone who is not 'all there'.
SCRIMP AND SAVE	Make do with much less, the opposite of being wasteful.
Scruff	Untidy, hence 'scruffy', see also ragamuffin, 'erb, tyke.
Scruff of the neck	Caught by, apprehended by, escaped by the scruff means having a narrow escape.
Scrumping	Pinching apples.

Scrumptious	Delicious.
Scullery	An area or room near the kitchen, now called a utility room.
Sculling	Propelling a small boat by one oar pivoted in a notch in the transom.
Seeing a new moon through glass	Is said to be unlucky, not seeing it through glass is lucky, turn the pennies over in your pocket and you'll be rich. (Note: the wearing of spectacles and glasses also applies).
SEEING THRU' TWO PANES OF GLASS	Wearing spectacles, or glasses. See above.
See-saw Margery Dawe	*'We shall have a new Master,'* a nursery rhyme usually sung whilst pushing a child on a swing, or rocking them in a cradle.
Send a wire	Send a telegram.
Set sail	Set off, embark, start a journey, not necessarily in a sailing boat.
Shambolic	Utter chaos, a way of describing a shambles of a scene or situation.
Shanks' pony	To go by Shanks' pony is to walk rather than take the bus.
Shifty	Unsure, unpredictable, not one's usual self.
Shimmy	A shirt or chemise, and what a wobbly castor wheel on a shopping trolley does.
Shilly shally	Go slow, meander, prevaricate, backslide.
Shirty	Annoyed with somebody, or them getting shirty with you.
Shite hawk	A scavenger, eats anything.
SHIVER ME' TIMBERS	Shaken to the core, shiver with fright. e.g. as a great wave can shake a wooden ship.
Shooting a line	Self aggrandisement, used to make a favourable impression, bragging.
Show a leg	The order to wake up and put a leg over the side of the bed to prove it.
SHRAMMED	Feeling very cold, chilled to the bone.
SHUFTI	Take a look, take a dekko, have a look see.
Shut yer cake 'ole	A none too polite way of saying shut up.

Shy	Fling or throw, e.g. have a throw at, a cock shy.
Siding with the angels	Making sure you are always on the right or winning side, self righteousness.
Simmer down	Cool it!
Sirens	Were used for sounding an 'alert' or air-raid warning.
SKEW WHIFF	Out of true, lopsided, twisted, distorted.
SKEDADDLE	Buzz off, scram, scarper, get lost.
Skint	Broke, without a bean.
Skinny as a rake	Lean, lanky, a bean pole.
Skivvy	Menial tasks, and the person who carries them out.
Skive off	Get out of doing something by bunking off.
Skulduggery	Trickery, unscrupulous behaviour, deviousness.
Slapdash	Untidy, no finesse, done in haste and looks like it.
Sleep tight	Often said without knowing its origin, it is a reminder to tighten the ropes under an Elizabethan mattress.
Slick, slick dick	Smart, smooth, e.g. slick your hair back using either Brylcreem or Brilliantine. Adept at doing something.
SLING YOUR HOOK	An order to leave, go away, get lost, buzz off, beat it.
Sloping shoulders	Ducks, shirks or avoids taking any responsibility whatsoever.
SLOW, EASY AND COMFORTABLE	And 'more haste less speed', two of Father's recipes for longevity.
Smooching, or smoochy woochy	Kissing, caressing, petting or slow close dancing.
Smuts	Getting covered with black sooty sticky stuff, puffing out of a steam train in a tunnel with the window down, or from a paddle steamer if you were up on deck on the down wind side.
Snake belt	A simple silver clasp in the shape of a snake, all the rage on boys' elasticated trouser belts.
SNAZZY	Smartly dressed, or wearing a smart outfit.
Sniffle	'A bit of a cold', having a runny nose.

Snivelling	Whining, whinging, a juvenile way of complaining with sniffs, frequent tears and a runny nose.
Snoopers	Unpopular officials and civilian 'whistleblowers' active in wartime.
Snooty	Aloof, haughty, nose in the air, act as though superior.
Snug as a bug in a rug	Warm, cosy and contented.
Square meal	A good meal, satisfying nourishing and sufficient.
SOLDIER'S WIND	Doing something with the benefit of a soldier's wind is to do it easily, like sailing with the wind on the beam.
SOFT SOAP	Persuasion by flattery, to gain support, confidence or coercion to do something.
Sold a pup	A poor quality useless purchase, see also swizz.
Sourpuss	Not a nice person to know, one who sours each thought and every word they say.
Sour grapes	Resentful of something you disagree with, or dislike.
Sou'wester	A rain proof hat that can be worn in a gale, can also mean a gale.
SPAM	SPiced hAM, American tinned ham, sliced and fried a treat at the end of WW2.
SPEED MERCHANT	Driving at excessive speeds, a road hog. What Father said every time when being overtaken in the Austin 7.
Spick and span	Clean, tidy and smart, not a speck of dust anywhere, and ready for inspection.
Spiffing	Super, superb, jolly good, top hole, swell.
Spills	Tightly twisted sheets of paper/newspaper used to light fires and smokers pipes, saved matches which were in short supply during the war. Also means minor accidents with bikes and cars.
Spill the beans	Reveal the contents of a secret, blab out the truth, betray confidentiality.
Spinning a yarn	Telling a tale or a story with verbal embellishment.
SPITHEAD AND THE SOLENT	Famous areas of sea off Portsmouth and Gosport, used for regattas, Cowes Week, sea-trials, and Royal Naval Reviews.
Splendiferous	A cut above splendid.
SPONDULIX	Another word for money.

Spot on	Exactly right, correct answer, accurate, on target.
Sprucer	Someone who can lead you up the garden path, and cannot be relied upon to be telling the truth, a con-man, a trickster.
SPRUCE UP	Wash and brush up, look one's best, improve one's appearance, to smarten up.
Squiffy	Drunk, tiddly, or not quite straight in the geometric sense, skew wiff.
Stair rods	A downpour of rain coming down in straight lines.
Stamping grounds	Old familiar places with well trodden paths, old haunts.
Stand offish	Aloof in a posh sort of way, unfriendly, portraying superiority, set apart.
Steamed up	Agitated, in a tizzy, upset, cross, in a two and eight.
Step on it	An instruction to go faster, accelerate, get a move on.
Step on the gas	Ditto.
Stingy	Pronounced 'stin-gee', mean, 'min-gee', ungenerous, measly, penny pinching'.
Stinkpot	Someone who smells badly, 'Smelly Nelly', and 'BO Bob'.
STIRRUP PUMP	A simple easy to use device to put out fires. Used extensively to extinguish incendiary bombs during the war, and still in use today, e.g. chimney fires.
Stone cold	Having the characteristics of a stone, e.g. cold, dead, stone deaf, or emphasising that it should be hot, e.g. this tea is stone cold.
Stone cold sober	The opposite of being drunk.
Stone the crows	An expression of surprise at the unexpected, or being nonplussed, incredulity.
Stony silence	Dead quiet, not a sound, you could hear a pin drop, as quiet as a morgue, or a graveyard.
STOP ME AND BUY ONE	The cry of the Wall's Ice Cream man and the slogan painted on the side of his three wheeled bicycle cart.
Straight up	'Honestly, its true', speaking the truth, honest Indian.
Strike a light	Expression of surprise, disbelief or enlightenment.
Stumped	Unable to answer or respond, nonplussed.

Stump up	Pay up, pay your debts reluctantly, forced to pay.
Superduper	Absolutely fabulous, spiffing, out of this world.
Swap me Bob	Exclamation of surprise.
Swank	Showing off, pretending to be 'posh', pretentious.
Swan about	Acting and looking as though doing something purposeful.
Swanning off	Avoid doing what you are expected to do, doing a bunk, bunking off, getting out of doing something. Same as sloping off.
Swell	American slang for fine, dandy, ok, super, 'great'.
Swells	Posh people, 'the well to do' e.g. the song - *'We're a couple of swells, we live in the best hotels'*.
Sweet FA (Fanny Adams)	Absolutely nothing at all.
Swig	A brief quaff of the ale, and any other drink come to that, e.g. take a swig out of the bottle.
Swim with the tide	Go along with whatever everyone else is doing, playing it safe, siding with the angels.
Swindle	A shady deal, dishonest deceitful, obtain by false pretences, e.g. by a swindler.
Swinging the lead	Shirking a duty, getting out of doing things, do very little or nothing at all.
Swish	Smart, fashionable, stylish, a la mode, trendy.
SWIZZ, SWIZZLE	A swindle, a fraud, tricked.

That's the Ticket!

Tables	'Tables' or 'times tables' were multiplication tables that had to be learnt by heart at school, often with the help of Wightman's Multiplication Tables, a small book with a brick red cover.
TA EVERSO	Thank you very much.
Ta ta	Cheerio, goodbye, bye bye.
Take a breather	Have a rest, take five, take a break, relax for a bit.
Take a leaf out of someone else's book	Take someone else's good idea and use it, following someone else's example.
Take off	Mimic.
Take on, or take on so	Undertake to do something, or to be upset by someone, e.g. 'don't take on so'.
Taken down a peg or two	Told off, have your rank or status reduced, put in your place.
Taken up	Started something like a sport or pastime, e.g. golf.
Taken with	Influenced by, attracted to.
TAKE THE WIND OUT OF THEIR SAILS	Stopping someone in their tracks, getting the better of someone, one upmanship.
(For many more takes and takens)	See Brewer's Dictionary of Phrase and Fable.
Tanner	Sixpence.
TATS	Going out to the shops, for a walk, taking the baby 'tats', a nice little 'outing'.
Tayters, ta-ters	Nonsense, a load of rubbish, or short for potatoes, e.g. 'I'll mash the tayters'.
Teasy weasy, easy peasey	Said when taunting or teasing someone, also the name of a music-hall character.

Teensy weensy	Tiny in childspeak.
Telling fibs	Little white lies, untruths, telling porkies.
Ten league boots	Large outsize boots.
Ten to the dozen	Going at speed or in haste, going at a rate of knots.
That's the rub	That's the problem, therein lies the problem, that's the trouble.
THAT'S THE TICKET or sometimes **JUST THE TICKET**	Just right, just what was wanted, making the correct decision, You're doing OK, e.g. giving encouragement.
Ten a penny	Plentiful and cheap.
The balloon's gone up	News of imminent danger in wartime, or a battle or attack that has already started.
The Beano	A popular weekly comic, along with the Dandy and Hotspur.
THE BIRD MAN	Clem Sohn made a gallant attempt to 'fly' like a bird above Portsmouth Airport in May 1936.
THE DOG'S SHELF	The floor.
The 'doings'	The name given to a 'thing' you can't remember the name of, called a Cadigan.
THE FLEET'S LIT UP	The infamous words slurred by a 'squiffy' commentator during the 1937 BBC Outside Broadcast describing the Review of the Fleet at Spithead.
The Home Front	All those wartime activities carried out by the civilian population that contributed to the war effort, e.g. The Home Guard (Dad's Army).
The Home Guard	Dad's Army, the LDVs.
The Home Service	The only BBC wireless programme during wartime.
The Ink Spots	A deep voiced vocal American Group, well known for singing the song *'Bless you for being an angel'*.
The long and the short of it	Stripped to the bone, getting to the point, getting down to brass tacks, no frills.
THE LONG LEG	Ask a sailor or yachtsman to explain this one!
THE NEVER NEVER	Was the popular name in the early days for deferred payments, hire purchase and credit agreements.

THE NEVER NEVER LAND	Where lost boys and Indians went, J.M.Barrie's Peter Pan. See also Arzums.
The Old Bill	A respectful name given to the Police and 'Bobbies' on the beat.
Thetis	A submarine disaster in 1939.
THE TROLLEY BUS	A new fangled double decker bus with long poles on its roof to reach the overhead power cables. Doing the tight U-turn at the Dockyard gates required the poles to be lowered and the turn completed by battery power. This complicated de-and re-coupling procedure was a spectator sport for boys young and old.
The Valeta	A popular dance at hops.
The Victory class	The classic 'one design' class of yacht sailed and raced exclusively by the Portsmouth Sailing Club.
The War Effort	Determination by the civilian population to win the war on the Home Front by working hard in pursuit of a common purpose. Aided by patriotism and propaganda.
The whys and the wherefores	Going into detail, giving a full explanation.
There's no such thing as can't	Said by Father giving encouragement to anyone about to give up trying.
Thing a me bob, or jig or thingy	Something you can't quite remember the name of. See oojameeflick, and cadigans.
Thinking cap	Putting on your thinking cap is to concentrate the mind and solve a difficult question.
Three sheets to the wind	Drunk.
Through thick and thin	Encountering and overcoming adversity along the way towards achieving a goal, a difficult journey.
Thruppence and a thripney bit	Three pennies in old money. A three penny piece.
Tickled pink	Take one's fancy, highly amused, laughed until red in the face.
Ticklers	Cigarettes, fags.
Tiddly	Slightly drunk, squiffy, or inebriated.
TIDE YOU OVER	Helping out by providing a short term solution. e.g. here's a fiver to tide you over.

TIGHT AS A TICK	Very drunk, and merrily so.
Tight fisted	Being mean, not spending money, frugal.
Tin hats	Drunk in a general sense.
Tipping it down	Raining hard, raining cats and dogs, coming down like stair rods.
Tipsy	Slightly drunk, merry.
Titbits	Tiny morsels, small pieces of special interest, enticing, food or information, tittle tattle, and gossip.
Titbits	A magazine containing all of the above, plus bits and pieces of news, gossip.
Titch	A short, small, tiny person. was called Titch. Titch replacing their first name, e.g. 'Titch' Wilson, also known as 'nipper'.
TITFER	Hat.
Tit for tat	Give as good as you get, respond in equal measures, a fair exchange.
Tizzy	Getting all hot and bothered, hot under the collar. Upset, e.g. 'Being in a tizzy'.
Tizz woz	An altercation, a two and eight, the outcome of being in a tizzy.
To blab	Reveal a secret, spill the beans, blow the gaff.
To blub	To cry, hence crying is blubbing or blubbering, and a blubber baby is a baby that cries incessantly.
To blurt out	Inadvertently or deliberately say out loud something which should not have been said, e.g. the truth, a secret.
TOFF	Well to do, a posh person, an upper class 'gent'.
Toffee nosed	Stuck up, pompous, nose stuck up in the air.
Togs	Gear, clothes for a particular purpose, e.g. cricket togs.
To a 't'	Down to a 't', correct in every detail, or he took him off to a 't', e.g. to mimic.
To eat humble pie	Reluctantly confess and have to admit you were wrong.
To give one's eye teeth for something	Willing to give anything to get what you want, to set one's cap at it.

To give the top brick off the chimney for it	Willing to pay a high price for something you really want.
To have no truck with it	To have no dealings with, nor anything to do with something.
To kingdom come	A long way away, e.g. send him to kingdom come, or gone to kingdom come.
Tomfoolery	A merry prank, larking about.
Tommy rot	Piffle, balderdash, rubbish and nonsense.
TOODLE DO, OR TOODLE PIP	A cheery farewell.
TOOSIE PEGS	A child's first set of teeth.
Top drawer	Of the finest quality, to be put only in the top drawer, the best. See bottom drawer.
Top hole or top notch	Excellent, well done, splendid, superior, second to none.
Topsy turvy	All upside down, a mess, a pickle, higgledy piggledy.
Totting up	Adding up, calculating, counting, e.g. counting the cost.
Touch and go	Dodgy, without certainty, doubtful, risky, chancy.
Tow or toe the line	Obey orders, follow the rules, come into line, conformity with what is required.
TRAFFICATOR	An illuminated direction indicator that pointed like a finger and used on cars before flashing ones.
Treading water	Having to work hard just to keep afloat or standing still.
Trice	In a fraction of a second, it happened in a trice.
Trick cyclist	Psychiatrist.
TRIPE	Nonsense, talking rubbish, baloney, bilge.
TROTS	Effect of an upset tummy, the 'runs', and also rows of yacht moorings.
Trucking, or to truck something	Moving something by means of a wheel.
Trumped up	A case founded on false pretences or premises, e.g. 'a trumped up charge'.
TRUNKS	Bathing shorts for boys, see also 'bathers'.

TTFN	Ta ta for now, from the BBC comedy ITMA.
Tuppenny	Used when addressing a young or small person, often referring to them as 'my little tupney'.
Turkhead	A Gosportian.
TURKTOWN	Another name for Gosport.
Turn in	Go to bed, get some kip.
Turn the tables	Change losing into winning, turn misfortune into good fortune.
Turn turtle	Turn upside down by going sideways, e.g. rolling a canoe.
Tut tut	Said as a mild reprimand.
Twerp	A naked lady (dict. def.) now used to describe a silly or stupid person.
TWICER	A trickster, a fraud, not to be trusted, a conman.
Twiddle	Fiddle with, make minor adjustments, e.g. twiddle the knobs of a radio.
TWIGGED	Cottoned on, or onto, guessed correctly, saw the answer, the penny has dropped.
Twister	A fraudster, a trickster, untrustworthy, see twicer.
Twit	Stupid, a nincompoop.
Twoddle	Just plain nonsense, often called 'twiddle twoddle'.
Two a penny	Plentiful, and cheap.
TWO HOURS BEFORE HIGH WATER THE TIDE STARTS RUNNING TO THE WEST	A local navigational maxim for the Solent and Spithead to be learnt by heart.
Two pennies worth	Getting a word in edgeways irrespective of its worth, having your say.

'Up the Wooden Hill'

Um and ah	Prevaricate, slow to make a decision, said when trying to think of the answer, or what to say.
UMPTEENTH	Describing an indefinite number of times you've lost count e.g. 'for the umpteenth time'.
Under the weather	Ill, unwell, not feeling up to it, not 100%, one degree under.
UNCLE SAM	Someone to confide in, or seek guidance from, mentor, counsellor, (**Everyone needs an Uncle Sam!**)
Up a gum tree	Well and truly stuck, in a spot of bother.
Up and a downer	A rough sea passage, or two people having a row or altercation.
'Up armzees followed by 'skin a rabbit'	The two stages of having a vest pulled over your head when being undressed for bed.
Up's a daisy	Said when about to lift a small child.
Up hill and down dale, or dell	All over the place, e.g. we looked for it everywhere, or a long tramp in the countryside.
Up in arms	Cross, making a protest, to be actively involved in a dispute.
Up is north, down is south, (and out) east & west are across	Agreed by general consensus, custom and practice.
Upper crust	The upper class, at the top of the pile, socially superior.
Up the creek	In difficulty or trouble, often followed by, without a paddle which is worse.
Up the garden path	Surreptitiously misleading someone into believing something that will never happen, giving someone false hopes. Led astray, misled, misguided, bamboozled into something.

UP THE HILL	Climbing or going up Portsdown Hill, from the south. e.g. for a picnic. See also 'up the wooden hill'.
Up shot	The outcome, e.g. well the up shot of it all was.
Up the, or let's go up the (wherever)	Usually meant going out somewhere in a northerly direction, e.g. up to Fareham, down is south, (and down is out!)
Up there	Refers to being 'brainy' or not, you've either got it or you haven't, e.g. he has nothing much 'up there'.
UP THE WOODEN HILL	Said by Fathers at bed time when climbing the stairs with a child.
Urchin	Ragamuffin, a poor and uncared-for child.
US'ENS	Us as distinct from them'ens, our group, our gang or our family.
Utility	Used in wartime, it referred to a no frills design that fulfilled its function well and at a reasonable cost, from railway engines to pencils.
Use it, or lose it	Exactly what it says, e.g. the sense of smell.

'V for Victory'

VAMOOSE   Push off, clear off, hop it.

VERA LYNN   The Forces Sweetheart. See *'Keep smiling through'*.

V FOR VICTORY   The Morse code, three dots and a dash. The first four
                     notes of Beethoven's fifth symphony. The Churchillian
                     two fingered V-sign were patriotic and morale boosting
                     sounds, slogans and symbols used during WW2.

VICKY VERKY   A popular alternative to saying vice versa, first heard in a
                     BBC comedy series.

VIROL   A ghastly, viscous, evil tasting tonic for kids, made from
                     cod liver oil, second only to Californian syrup of figs.

'Well I'll go to the bottom of our stairs'

Warm as toast	Comfortably warm, "I'm nice and warm thank you".
WARM THE COCKLES OF YOUR HEART	Something that warms and comforts, e.g., a pleasant experience, hot toddy, brandy.
Waxing lyrical	Extrapolation of a subject by eloquent verbosity.
'WE ARE THE OVALTINEYS'	'Happy Girls & Boys' - the jingle for the Ovaltinees Club sung on Radio Luxemburg.
Wearing a green jacket	Feigning a lack of knowledge, not revealing that you knew all along.
Wearing a dunces' hat	A tall, white, conical hat with a 'D' on it that 'duffers' were made to wear in class, and so drawing everybody's attention to the fact that they were 'dim'.
WELL I'LL GO TO THE BOTTOM OF OUR STAIRS	Said as an expression of utter amazement.
WE'LL I'M BLOWED	Fancy that, well would you believe it, well I never, well I never did, incredulity, taken aback, taken completely by surprise, amazed.
Wet behind the ears	Someone with a lot still to learn, lacking experience.
Wet week	Refers to someone who is a drip, weak, and dismal, can also mean a very long week.
Wet your whistle	Quench your thirst.
What a turn up for the book	A verbal outcry to a pleasing or surprising outcome.
What a wopper	Referring to a large one.
What cher! or wot ho!	Hello, a friendly greeting.
Whatever next	A surprise event, followed by another perhaps.
What price so and so	A way of expressing an interest and surprise, at rumour, gossip, or tit bit.

Whatsmore	'And in addition to that', additionally, moreover, besides.
When Adam was a lad	Emphasising that it all took place a long time ago.
WHIPPERSNAPPER	'You little whippersnapper', said in mild admonishment to a child having committed some minor misdemeanour.
Whistle and ride	Get a move on, hurry up, get yer skates on.
WHITE HORSES	Wave tops breaking white, a sign and portent of increasing winds, and stormy weather.
Whoops, or whoopsy	Pardon me, excuse me I've made a mistake, or said on stumbling, unsteadiness or dropping something.
Whoops a daisy	Said when you or a child stumbles, and as above.
WINCARNIS	A popular livation, or livener, taken as a daily tonic and 'pick me up', Mother's favourite.
WINDBAG	A person who has a lot to say, and takes a long time saying it.
Winceyette	The best material for making warm clothes, like pyjamas and blankets.
Wits end	Nonplussed, flummoxed, floored, unable to find a solution, at the end of your tether.
With tooth and nail	Fight with everything you've got, fight with all your might and with every possible means.
Wizard	Cool, super, super duper, fabulous, top hole, stupendous, brill.
Wizard prang	Doing or done something special, although in the RAF a 'prang' usually meant crashing an aircraft.
Wonky	Not straight, out of true, bent, skew whiff.
Worse things happen at sea	Whatever has happened could have been a lot worse.
Wouldn't put it past him/her	Wouldn't be surprised if he/she did so and so, a person known to do the unexpected or the unusual.
Wow!	Expression of amazement, e.g. wow! what a whopper.
WOZZER	Was she? Referring to, or meaning a she, e.g. 'wozzer' telling the truth!".
WOZZ I?	Was I?

Wreck of the Hesperus   Looking a mess, thoroughly untidy in appearance, dishevelled, e.g. 'she arrived at the party looking like the Wreck of the Hesperus', or as though she had been dragged through a hedge backwards.

Wringer   A household appliance with wooden rollers used for squeezing water out of wet washing called a 'mangle', eventually replaced by the spin drier.

'You'll never find pockets in a shroud'

Yackety yack	Endless chat or verbiage.
Ye daft ha'peth	You silly billy, you soppy ha'peth, you soppy date.
YIMPBEGOMP	A familiar way of describing someone who has done something daft silly or stupid.
YONKS	A long time, taking ages, taking forever.
You mark my words	Heed what I have to say, you just see if I'm right. You'll find out I'm right in the long run, a prophetic edict by Father (like me coming unstuck eventually).
YOU'LL COP IT	Whatever you are about to do or have just done will get you into trouble for which you will be punished.
YOU'LL NEVER FIND POCKETS IN A SHROUD	A saying that should need no explanation.
You're for the high jump	You're in big trouble, you're in for it, you've got it coming to you.
Your number's up	Sussed out, found out, time it came to an end, it's over, time to quit (**never has a truer word been spoken!**)

Except for...

'Zoot Suit'

Zany

Crazy, one who 'acts the goat', a screwball, see also 'Hellzapoppin'.

ZOOT SUIT

Men's long frock coats and tapered trousers that were worn in the 1930's and later by 'hepcats' and followers of 'swing', and then there were thick crepe-soled shoes called 'brothel creepers'.

Zombie

Being half alive, or half dead, not being with it, sometimes referred to as 'zombied' when someone is slow to respond.

Latecomers

- that slipped in through the back door by the skin of their teeth

To nab	To nab someone is to catch, collar or apprehend them.
The Nab Tower	A sort of Fort in the sea off the eastern end of the Isle of Wight that can be seen from Southsea 'Front' on a clear day.
The Street Singer	Arthur Tracy whose plaintive voice brought many to tears for his heartrending songs such as *'It's my Mother's birthday today'*, *'Keep calling me sweetheart'* and *'When the poppies bloom again'*.
A pot mess	Grandfather Pap's special word for a mix up, problem or difficulty.
So and so	Used when referring to a person whose name you cannot remember, see Cadigans.
For the full list of Cadigans	See page 42 in part two.
A so and so	Refers to a particular person who has done something disreputable, dishonest, annoying or unpopular.
On tenterhooks	To be anxious, nervous, and apprehensive, about something about to happen.
The Briney and the Oggin	The sea or the ocean.
Learning the ropes	Learning the ins and outs of a new job or situation.
Getting spliced	Getting married.
Spit and polish	What you did to your boots and other bits of kit when preparing for an inspection, referred to in the services as 'bullshit'.
Working your fingers to the bone	Hard work for little pay, e.g. in a corset factory.
T'was on the good ship Venus	By God you should have seen us!

Airs and graces	A derogatory remark about a person acting as though they were much more important than they really were.
Belongings	One's personal possessions.
Little 'un	A small young person, see titch, nipper.
Elocution	Private tuition for speaking clear, correct and proper!
A fuss pot	Constantly and annoyingly, pernickety and fastidious.
Cubby hole	A nook, cranny or small repository in which to put anything of the right size you care to mention.
Landlubber	Some one who doesn't sail the seas, for what ever reason.
A ditty	A favourite little tune or song, e.g. *'She was a dear little dicky bird, tweet tweet tweet she went'*.
A ditty box or bag	Any small box or canvas bag with a lock in which to keep personal belongings.
Red handed	Caught in the act of committing a crime.
Jack Tar or jolly jack tar	Old nicknames for a sailor.
A washout	An event that had to be cancelled, curtailed or abandoned, e.g. a rained off summer fete.
Sloshed	Drunk.

Ad infinitum

Some Sources of Further Reference

Origins of 'Pompey' and 'Turktown'

The now legendary and varied answers to why **Portsmouth** became known as 'Pompey' and **Gosport** became known as 'Turktown' still provoke controversy, and will continue to be prime topics for further research and debate on both sides of the Harbour.

The following sources are offered without prejudice.

'Pompey'

Good Old Pompey - but why? - Did Nelson ever say to our dearest Emma: See you in Pompey? - The Hampshire Magazine, September 1964, p. 16. Editor: Dennis Stevens.

The Portsmouth That Has Passed, With Glimpses of God's Port, - 'Poor Old Pompey' - Origin of this Pathetic Description, by William G. GATES, Ed. by F.J.H. Young, - 1904, 1987 Edition. Published by Milestone (Portsmouth) and the Portsmouth Evening News, ISBN 185-265-113.

From an obsolete website dated 20.07.98:
http://www.pompey.demon.co.uk/pompey.htm. page 1 of 3 - Origin of the Term 'Pompey' for Portsmouth - copies available from the Portsmouth Central Library, Local History Section.

Evening News: Origin of the Term 'Pompey' for Portsmouth - Dec 2.1933 p.3 col. 3. Oct 9 1934 p.6 col. 7. - Dec 9 1899 p. 3 col. 6. - Aug 24 1957 p. 2 cols. 2 and 3. **www.portsmouth.co.uk**

A dictionary of slang and unconventional English by Alan Partridge, 1949. p. 647.

The Portsmouth Society
email enquiries: mailbox@portsmouthsociety.org.uk
website: www.portsmouthsociety.org.uk

'Turktown'

Why Gosport Became Turktown, John Edgar MANN, in the series: 'Mann at Large', 'Hampshire - the County Magazine', Oct. 1993, pp. 44-45.

Why Turktown?, Margaret ROBERTS, The Gosport Society Newsletter, June 1995, pp. 5-6.

'Corner of a foreign field that is forever Turkish', Chris OWEN in the series 'Owen's Eye', The 'News', August 8th 2003.

The Gosport Society can be contacted by one of the following:

Gosport Society
PO Box No 188
Gosport, PO12 9AF
email: gosport.society@ntlworld.com

'Why Turktown'

A memory from the author:

Hearsay, when young, convinced us'ens who played on the southern banks of Forton Creek (which we called the 'Arzums'), that a number of Turkish sailors had been imprisoned nearby just inside the St Vincent boundary with the farm that bordered our gardens in Grove Road South.

They reportedly spent their days carving exquisitely detailed ships out of bone *(might one of these be the fine example of an English 'Man of War' HMS Lion, known to have been made from bone by prisoners of war during the Napoleonic era and which is now in Levens Hall, Cumbria?)*

T'was said, they were never released and subsequently died and were buried by the banks of Forton Creek. In spite of valiant efforts to reach the remains of the little cemetery and prove its existence, we were never able to penetrate the heavily barbed-wire fence that surrounded St.Vincent's perimeter in those far off days.

dfb.

General Reference

A Word in your Ear, Nigel REES, Collins, 2006.
6000 curious and everyday phrases explained.
ISBN 0-00-722087-1, 978-0-00-722087-8

Brewer's Dictionary of Phrase and Fable, revised by Adrian ROOM, Cassel,
16th Ed., 1999, revised 2004.
ISBN 0-304-35096-6 (hbk), 0-304-35873-8 (pbk)

Dictionary of Dockyard Language, compiled and illustrated by B. PATTERSON,
Portsmouth Royal Dockyard Historical Society.

Dictionary of Euphemisms, R.W. HOLDER, BCA/OUP, 1995.
How not to say what you mean. CN 1393

Dictionary of Idioms, Wordsworth Editions Ltd., 1993.
An alphabetical guide to colourful and peculiar phrases and expressions.
ISBN 1-85326-309-5

Mother Tongue, Bill BRYSON, Penguin Books Ltd., 1991.
A witty, irreverent but useful account of the peculiarities of the English language.
ISBN 978-0-14-014305-8.

Red Herrings and White Elephants, Albert JACK, Metro Publishing, 2004.
The origins of the phrases we use every day.
ISBN 1-84358-129-9

Shaggy Dogs and Black Sheep, Albert JACK, Penguin Books, PB 2006.
The origins of even more phrases we use everyday.
ISBN 10: 0-141 02425-9.   ISBN13: 978-0-141-02425-7

Ship's Miscellany, Michael O'Mara Books Limited 2003.
A guide to the Royal Navy of Jack Aubrey.
ISBN 1-84317-077-9

Ship to Shore, Peter D. JEANS, ABC-CLIO Inc., Oxford, England,
A dictionary of everyday words and phrases derived from the Sea. 1993.
ISBN 0-87436-717-4

www.wikipedia.com